I0455599

CONTENTS

CHAPTER 1

INTRODUCTION

Tarek Saadawi
Louis H. Jordan, Jr.
Vincent Boudreau

In recent years, the analysis of cyber security has moved into what one might call a series of second-generation conversations. The first generation, dominated by engineers and computer programmers, regarded the issue as primarily a technical matter, and sought responses from cyber threats mainly in the development of protective software and hardware design. In its early phases, cyber threats were primarily regarded as politically neutral, and without a great deal of economic motivation. Hence, how these threats were generated, and what social or political actors or systems directed these attacks, mattered little. Up-to-date anti-virus software and other protective technology were judged sufficient to protect both personal and public cyber assets against attack.

Several things have changed since those early conversations. First, and most obviously, technology has grown more complex and more networked. As our society demanded more interactive cyber systems, the danger of contamination across these systems has grown. Second, cyber attacks have become less economically or politically neutral than in previous generations. Evidence is mounting that both governments and insurgent groups are using cyber platforms as a way of mounting attacks. Threats to cyber security from economically motivated groups, and especially, increasingly well-organized criminal syndicates, are more advanced. Third, innovations in cyber technology each year make increasingly sophisticated cyber weapons more widespread. Moreover, as the market in malware evolves, the technology can be rented, making the threat more and more affordable. Finally, trends in technology development suggest that, generally, efforts to defend against cyber attacks will always be more expensive than efforts to develop new forms of attack. Over time, therefore, the possibility of developing purely technical solutions to the threats against cyber security seems dauntingly uneconomical, even if entirely technologically feasible.

There is a relentless struggle taking place in the cyber sphere as government and business spend billions attempting to secure sophisticated network and computer systems. Cyber attackers are able to introduce new viruses and worms capable of defeating many of our efforts. The military depends more on technological solutions than ever before. A cyber attack on military operations could be more devastating than the effects of traditional weaponry. Additionally, these attacks will come from an unseen adversary who will likely be unreachable for a counterattack or countermeasure. In this "Fifth" generation of warfare, the battlefield is everywhere, and everyone potentially becomes a combatant, which causes grave new questions in the areas of the law of war as well as national sovereignty. The U.S. military must work closer than ever before with the various agencies of government, business, and academia to understand the threat and develop various modes of fighting cyber attacks.

Where, then, has the discussion of cyber security turned? Some answers lie in reversing trends toward greater integration and increasing technological sophistication. As cyber threats diffuse across increas-

2

ingly connected networks, some have sought to counter them by developing lower-technology systems unintegrated with the larger cyber infrastructure, simply by having their own isolated cyber islands disconnected from the larger cyber systems. Others continue—as they must—to fight the war on a technological front, developing faster and more sophisticated ways of countering cyber threats. But for many, the evolution of cyber security requires a new and deeper understanding of the social, economic, and political dynamics that animate cyber terrorism and cybercrime. As with conventional security analysis, or efforts to decrease or frustrate criminal behavior more generally, we have begun to consider how the social forces that motivate and govern the generation of cyber threats can influence cyber security. By understanding how the market in criminal malware operates, or figuring out the dynamics that hold organized crime together, cyber security specialists can more effectively develop methods of staving off those threats. While the last several decades have perhaps encouraged us to think of cyber threats as programs, viruses, worms, spyware, and botnets, current conversation recalls that people—connected to one another in organizations or through networks, motivated by political or criminal concerns, living in societies and subject to laws—deploy these threats.

The tools of foreign policy, conventional security studies, criminology, sociology, and economic theory are all relevant to the analysis of these threats. Deterrence theory, for example, focuses on how to prevent people with capacity from acting to inflict harm. Game theory explores how different political objectives and modes of interaction—reassurance, recognition, security, and prestige—influence exchanges of threat or attack. But if useful, these analytic tools need now to navigate an entirely new landscape. How, for instance, can one deter an entity that thrives on the secrecy of an Internet identity? Are there ways of deterring cyber warriors who thrive on the prestige of making a bold cyber strike? Can we translate strategies designed to influence the behavior of nation-states (who must balance a range of goals that include their power, the stability of their regimes, and the well-being of their populations) to use against smaller networks, with neither citizens nor legal standing to worry about? In important and obvious ways, we cannot simply turn to the established works of social scientists for answers.

The problem, of course, is compounded by the technological side of things, and the fact that social scientists, computer scientists, engineers, and technicians have an uneven track record of working together to solve these problems (though in the current environment, work together they must). Does current technology allow us to deter a cyber attack credibly? If political strategy suggests a move from the existing, more defensive posture, to one that favors a proactive attack on insurgent or criminal organizations, what might such a weapon look like, and what are the broader implications of using offensive cyber weapons? As such questions illustrate, the solution to many of today's most pressing cyber threats (as well as those we can imagine emerging in the near and distant future) rests not in the realm of the social sciences, but in efforts to integrate lessons derived from those sciences into the design of technological work; the march of cyber technology needs to merge around politically informed strategies for the deployment of that technology. Hence, while cyber security once functioned mainly as a shield to deflect attacks, wherever they

4

came from and however they were directed, contemporary technological design must figure out both how to protect cyber assets, and how to identify, interdict, disrupt, and frustrate the organizations that mount attacks against them.

This book is designed as a way of entering this conversation. The chapters in this book were mainly presented as papers at the Cyber Infrastructure Protection 2011 conference at the City College of New York, in early-June 2011. At this conference, presenters were asked to think about the relationship between the technical and human elements of the threats to cyber security. The discussion was wide ranging, including experts in law, criminal behavior, international dynamics, and, of course, technical elements of cyber security. This book includes many of those papers, as well as several additional contributions. By presenting this work, more research and development of strategy toward a more integrated approach to cyber security, which borrows both from the fields of technology and engineering and from broader social scientific approaches, may take place.

OUTLINE OF THE BOOK

The book is divided into three main parts. Part I discusses the economic and social aspects of cyber security, covering the economics of malicious software and stolen data markets as well as the emergence of the civilian cyber warrior. Part II deals with laws and cybercrime, covering social and justice models for enhanced cyber security, and provides an institutional and developmental analysis of the data breach disclosure laws. Part II also provides solutions for the critical infrastructure that protect civil liberties and enhanced security, and explores the utility of open source data. Part III presents the technical aspects of the cyber infrastructure and presents monitoring for Internet service provider (ISP) grade threats as well as the challenges associated with cyber issues.

ECONOMICS AND SOCIAL ASPECTS OF CYBER SECURITY

The first two chapters in this book provide a framework for the economic and social aspects of cyber security. In Chapter 2, Thomas Holt explains how hackers utilize data from a sample of active, publicly accessible web forums that traffic in malware and personal information to consider the supply and demand for various types of malicious software and related cybercrime services which have a prospective economic impact on cybercrime campaigns against civilian and business targets. In order to explore and expand our understanding of the economics of cybercrime in general, this chapter utilizes a qualitative analysis of a series of threads from publicly accessible Russian web forums that facilitate the creation, sale, and exchange of malware and cybercrime services. The findings explore the resources available within this marketplace and the costs related to different services and tools. Using these economic data, coupled with loss metrics from various studies, this analysis considers the prospective economic impact of cybercrime campaigns against civilian and business targets. The findings provide insights into the market dynamics of cybercrime and the utility of various malware and attack services in the hacker community. In summary, this chapter explores the market for malicious software and cybercrime services in order to understand the price and availability of resources, as well as the relationship between the price paid for services and the cost experienced by victims of these crimes.

In Chapter 3, Max Kilger focuses on the civilian cyber warrior—who poses perhaps the most significant emerging threat to domestic and foreign critical infrastructures. Chapter 3 starts by providing some basic background for a schema that outlines six motivational factors that encourage malicious online behaviors.

The key concept is that perhaps for the first time in history, an everyday ordinary civilian can effectively attack a nation-state—in this case, through a cyber attack on some component of that nation-state's critical infrastructure. "Effectively" here means that the attack can cause significant widespread damage and has a reasonably high probability of success and a low probability of the perpetrator being apprehended. One of the first things that one might want to investigate in the chain of actions for a terrorist act is the initial starting point, where individuals begin thinking about and rehearsing in their minds the nature, method, and target for the terrorist attack. A key point for historical and social significance of the emergence of a civilian cyber warrior is the psychological significance of the event. The reassessment of the usual assumptions of the inequalities of the levels of power between nation-states and citizens establishes new relationships between institutions of society, government, and individuals.

An initial examination of the severity of physical attacks and cyber attacks that respondents feel are appropriate to launch against a foreign country bring both good news and bad news to the table. On the one hand, the vast majority of respondents select only responses that have minor or no consequences to the targeted foreign country. On the other hand, there are a nontrivial number of respondents who personally advocate the use of physical and cyber attacks against a foreign country that have some moderate to very serious consequences. While there is some comfort in the fact that expressing intentions to commit terrorist acts is only the first link in the behavioral chain from ideation to the execution of an attack, and bearing in mind that this is a scenario-based situation, even a small incidence of individuals who would consider some of the most serious acts is troubling. This suggests that the emergence of the civilian cyber warrior (and perhaps the physical attack counterpart) is an event to take into account when developing policies and distributing resources across national priorities to protect national critical infrastructures. Knowing the enemy can be a key element in gaining a comprehensive perspective on attacks against online targets.

LAW AND CYBERCRIME

Legal and cybercrime are explored in Part II of this book. In Chapter 4, Michael M. Losavio, J. Eagle Shutt, and Deborah Wilson Keeling argue that to change the game in cyber security, we should consider criminal justice and social education models to secure the highly distributed elements of the information network, extend the effective administration of justice to cybercrime, and embed security awareness and competence in engineering and common computer practice. Safety and security require more than technical protections and police response. They need a critical blend of these elements with individual practice and social norms. Social norms matched with formal institutions enhance public safety, including in the cyber realm. Informal and formal modes of controlling and limiting deviant behavior are essential for effective security.

Chapter 4 suggests that routine activity theory, opportunity theory, and displacement theory—frameworks for analyzing crime in communities—are ways to conceptualize and pattern the benefits of informal social control on cyber security. Routing Activity Theory (RAT) presents that, for cyber security, the analysis should equally consider the availability of suitable targets, a presence or lack of suitable guardians, and an increase or decrease in the number of motivated offenders—particularly those seeking financial gain or state advantage. Online social networks themselves suggest opportunities for the examination of RAT-based security promotion. Facebook, MySpace, and LiveJournal are online social networks that can promote cyber security within and without their domains. RAT can also be applied to criminal activity involving computing systems. Criminological principles to cyber security also relate to the use of criminal profiling and behavioral analysis. The reactive use of these techniques, much like the use of technical digital forensics in network settings, serves to focus an investigation and response in particular areas and on particular individuals. The proactive use of profiling can deter or prevent crime, such as drug courier profiling.

In Chapter 5, Melissa Dark considers the state data breach disclosure laws recently enacted in most states of the United States. Three reasons make the state data breach disclosure laws of interest: (1) the rapid policy growth; (2) the first instance of an informational regulation for information security; and, (3) the importance of these laws to prevent identity theft and to protect privacy. Technological advancements are changing the information security and privacy landscape considerably. Yet, these policies are blunt instruments not suited to careful excision of these ills. Some advocates of modifying existing laws assert that the outcome of data breach disclosure should be to motivate large-scale reporting so that data breaches and trends can be aggregated, which allows a more purposeful and defensive use of incident data.

In Chapter 6, Joshua Gruenspecht identifies some problems of identity determination that raise some of the most complicated unresolved issues in cyber security. Industry and government are pursuing a number of approaches to better identify communicants in order to secure information and other assets. As part of this process, some policymakers have suggested that fundamental changes to the way in which the Internet transmits identity information may be necessary. Authentication is "the process of establishing an understood level of confidence that an identifier refers to a particular individual or identity." Authentication often involves an exchange of information before some other transaction in order to ensure, to the extent necessary for the transaction at hand, that the sender of a stream of traffic is who he or she claims to be or otherwise has the attributes required to engage in the given transaction. Attribution is the analysis of information associated with a transaction or series of transactions to try to determine the identity of a sender of a stream of traffic. Information collection and analysis is the focus of attribution. This chapter focuses on authentication and attribution; two other issues closely relate to identity and are critical elements of any secure system: authorization and auditing. This chapter considers these problems and concludes that authentication-oriented solutions are more likely to provide significant security benefits and less likely to produce undesirable economic and civil liberties consequences.

In Chapter 7, George W. Burruss, Thomas J. Holt, and Adam M. Bossler focus on the value of open reporting for malware creation and distribution. The authors consider how this information combines with other measures to explore the country-level economic, technological, and social forces that affect the likelihood of malware creation. The chapter proposes that online repositories containing data on malicious software can be valuable to study the macro-level correlations of malware creation. The data for the dependent variable used for this study (MALWARE) came from an open source malware repository where individuals could post information obtained on malicious software. The data for the independent variables derive from the *CIA World FactBook* and from Freedom House, a nongovernmental agency that collects annual data on political freedom around the globe. The chapter concludes that the diverse and sophisticated threats posed by hackers and malicious software writers require significant investigation by both the technical and social sciences to understand the various forces that affect participation in these activities. The chapter suggests that there is a strong need for greater qualitative and quantitative examinations of hacker communities around the world. Research on hacker subcultures in the United States, China, and Russia suggests that there are norms, justifications, and beliefs that drive individual action.

CYBER INFRASTRUCTURE

In Chapter 8, Abhrajit Ghosh presents a comprehensive view of network security from several years of research conducted at Telcordia; in particular, the problem of monitoring large-scale networks for malicious activity. The goal of the developed system is to detect various types of network traffic anomalies that could be caused by Distributed Denial of Service (DDoS), spamming, Internet protocol (IP) address spoofing, and botnet activities. Currently, three types of anomaly detectors are provided to collect data and generate alerts: (a) Volume Anomaly Detectors; (b) Source Anomaly Detectors; and, (c) Profile Anomaly Detectors. The goal of the source anomaly detectors is to identify instances of source IP address spoofing in observed flows. Here data for the monitored ISP is acquired via NetFlow/sFlow data feeds from three flow agents. The profile anomaly detectors can detect any behavioral anomalies pertaining to hosts within the monitored network.

One profile anomaly detector that is currently part of the system can identify potential spammers using flow data and spammer blacklists. The Telcordia system incorporates an efficient real-time volume anomaly detector designed to give early warning of observed volume anomalies. The volume anomaly detector operates by considering a near-term moving window of flow records when computing traffic travels to a destination address. The system incorporates a correlation engine that correlates alerts generated by the different types of anomaly detectors. A significant issue with many anomaly detection-based approaches is their potentially high false-positive rate. The correlation engine component is designed to reduce the possibility of generating false-positives. Finally, the use of an alert correlation component is valuable to a network operator who would be very interested in lowering false-positive rates.

The goal of Chapter 9, written by Stuart Starr, is to explore the state-of-the-art in our ability to assess cyber issues. To illuminate this issue, the author presents a manageable subset of the problem. Using that decomposition, he identifies candidate cyber policy issues that warrant further analysis and identifies and illustrates candidate Measures of Merit (MoMs). Subsequently, Starr characterizes some of the more promising existing cyber assessment capabilities that the community is employing. That discussion is followed by an identification of several cyber assessment capabilities that are necessary to support future cyber policy assessments. The chapter concludes with a brief identification of high priority cyber assessment efforts to pursue.

PART I:

ECONOMICS AND SOCIAL ASPECTS
OF
CYBER SECURITY

CHAPTER 2

EXPLORING THE ECONOMICS
OF THE MALICIOUS SOFTWARE MARKET

Thomas J. Holt

This research was sponsored by the National Institute of Justice, Award No. 2007-IJ-CX-0018 (August 2007-November 2009). The points of view within this document are those of the author and do not necessarily represent the official position of the U.S. Department of Justice.

INTRODUCTION

The growth and function of malicious software markets have caused a shift in the way that hackers use and access malware with varying degrees of skill. Specifically, web forums allow individuals to purchase access to sophisticated malicious software to victimize vulnerable systems and individuals and to sell the data they illegally obtain for a profit. Those with limited technical capabilities can utilize products sold in these markets to engage in attacks, while individuals with greater skill can generate a profit by providing access to their infrastructure and resources. While researchers are constantly exploring these markets to identify emerging threats, few have considered the actual economic conditions that affect the market, including the costs and benefits for offenders, and the losses incurred by affected victim computers. This qualitative study utilizes data from a sample of active publicly accessible web forums that traffic in malware and personal information to determine: the supply and demand for various types of malicious software and related cybercrime services; the offenders' costs associated with multiple forms of attacks; and the prospective economic impact of cybercrime campaigns against civilian and business targets. The findings will benefit computer security practitioners, law enforcement, and the intelligence community by exploring the market dynamics and scope of the underground economy for cybercrime.

OVERVIEW

As technology increasingly permeates all facets of modern life, the risks posed by cyber attacks have increased dramatically.[1] Hackers target all manner of systems around the world in order to steal information, compromise sensitive networks, and establish launch points for future attacks.[2] In fact, evidence suggests that the number of computer security incidents has increased as more countries connect to the Internet.[3] Many of these attacks stem from computer hackers living in China, Russia, and Eastern Europe.[4] A sizeable proportion of these actors utilize malicious software, or malware, to automate various aspects of an attack.[5]

Malicious software, including viruses, Trojan horse programs, and various other tools, simplify or automate portions of a compromise, making it possible to engage in more sophisticated or complex intrusions beyond the true skills of the attacker.[6] In addition, the emergence of botnet malware, which combines multiple aspects of existing malware into a single program, enables hackers to establish stable networks of infected computers around the world.[7] These botnets can engage in attacks ranging from the distribution of spam, denial of service attacks, and network scanning. The growth of botnet malware in the computer underground has revolutionized malware, leading individuals to lease out their infrastructure to the larger population of semi-skilled hackers to engage in attacks.[8]

The evolution of malware has led to the formation of an online marketplace for the sale and distribution of malicious software, stolen data, and hacking tools.[9] These markets largely operate in forums and Internet Relay Chat (IRC) channels in Russia and Eastern Europe and enable hackers to buy or sell various tools and services to facilitate attacks against all manner of targets. Few studies have, however, considered the impact of these markets on the economics of cybercrime for both victims and offenders. For instance, the ability to purchase sophisticated malware may reduce the time an individual must invest in an attack, and diminish the requisite knowledge needed to hack.[10] In addition, limited research has considered the supply and demand for different services within the malware market, calling into question the perceived value of certain tools and attacks relative to other offenses. Finally, the lack of concrete loss metrics on the impact of cybercrime in both the public and private sector make it difficult to understand the profits a cybercriminal may acquire.

In order to explore these issues and expand our understanding of the economics of cybercrime in general, this chapter utilizes a qualitative analysis of a series of threads from publicly accessible Russian web forums that facilitate the creation, sale, and exchange of malware and cybercrime services. The findings explore the resources available within this marketplace and the costs related to different services and tools.

Using this economic data coupled with loss metrics from various studies, this analysis considers the prospective economic impact of cybercrime campaigns against civilian and business targets. The findings provide insights into the market dynamics of cybercrime and the utility of various malware and attack services in the hacker community.

HACKING, MALWARE MARKETS, AND THE ECONOMIC IMPACT OF CYBERCRIME

In order to examine malicious software markets, it is critical to first understand the general dynamics of the hacker community, whose members create and utilize malware. Hackers operate within a subculture that values profound and deep connections to technology.[11] This subculture is also a meritocracy, in which participants judge one another based on their capacity to utilize computer hardware and software in innovative ways.[12] Those who can devise unique tools and identify new vulnerabilities garner respect from their peers and develop a reputation for skill and ability within the subculture.

There are, however, a limited number of individuals with the knowledge or skill necessary to engage in truly sophisticated hacks and attacks.[13] A larger proportion of the hacker community has some demonstrable skill and can understand both the theory and mechanics behind an attack, but may not be able to create all the tools necessary to complete an attack on their own. Thus, they may seek out resources from those with greater skill in order to improve their capabilities. Similarly, a portion of the hacker community simply seeks to engage in attacks or applications of hacking without developing the requisite knowledge necessary to complete the act.[14] These actors are referred to as "script kiddies," because they try to acquire malicious software and use these programs without understanding the full functionality or processes affected.

The variation in skill and ability within the hacker community, coupled with a strong desire for the free flow of information, led hackers to trade and distribute tools and information on and offline regularly.[15] In the 1980s and 1990s, individuals would often barter for new resources, whether through trading stolen information or credentials, bulletin board system (BBS) access, or other valuable resources.[16] The creation of electronic payment systems and changes in the popularity of technology and information sharing, however, has engendered the growth of online markets where hackers can sell tools and data.[17]

Examinations of these marketplaces indicate that hackers can now buy and sell resources to facilitate attacks or information acquired after a compromise. Hackers regularly sell credit card and bank accounts, pin numbers, and supporting customer information obtained from victims around the world in lots of tens or hundreds of accounts.[18] Individuals also offer cashout services to obtain funds from electronic accounts or automated teller machine systems (ATMs) offline, as well as checking services, to validate whether an account is active, as well as any available balances. Spam- and phishing-related services are also available in Internet relay chat (IRC) channels, including bulk email lists to use for spamming and email injection services to facilitate responses from victims.[19] Some sellers also offer Distributed Denial of Service (DDoS) services and web hosting on compromised servers.[20]

These studies clearly demonstrate the burgeoning marketplace for hacking tools and stolen data, and some insights into the costs of goods and services. Few, however, have considered how the fee structures and pricing for malware and data services may affect offender decisionmaking. For instance, it is unclear how much an individual may earn from a spam, denial of service, or malware infection campaign relative to his or her initial investment. This is due to the substantial difficulty in obtaining information about the losses to individual and corporate victims of cybercrime.[21] Intrusions and attacks are often unreported to law enforcement, particularly in corporate settings, because businesses may not recognize, or may cover up, the problem to minimize customer concerns.[22] Similar issues arise in estimating the losses individual citizens experience due to cybercrime. Many home users may not recognize that their computer has been compromised or perceive that the incident may not be investigated or taken seriously by law enforcement.[23]

As a consequence, there are few official statistics available on the prevalence of cybercrimes reported to law enforcement agencies.[24] For instance, this information is not provided in the Federal Bureau of Investigation's (FBI) annual Uniform Crime Reports, and few industrialized nations report cybercrime through a central government outlet.[25] There are also a limited number of outlets that report the economic impact of computer intrusions and cyber attacks. This is due to the difficulty in accurately estimating the costs related to clean and mitigate an infection or patch all affected systems.[26] The variation in the impact of an attack also makes it difficult to determine appropriate loss metrics. For example, it is unclear whether the estimated financial harm of a DDoS attack is based on the prospective loss of revenue from prospective customers or losses to employee productivity.

As a consequence, data on the costs of cybercrime are largely generated by small samples of corporations willing to provide information based on attacks within their environments.[27] Similarly, the Internet Crime Complaint Center is one of the few outlets that provides consistent statistics on the economic impact of certain forms of cybercrime victimization in the general population.[28] The reported estimates use only self-reported victimization as the basis for examination. Thus, it is unknown how common these offenses are in the general population or how the variation in losses affect individual behavior while online.

In light of the significant gap in our knowledge of the economics of cybercrime for both offenders and victims, this chapter will explore this issue using a qualitative analysis of 909 threads from 10 active web forums in Russia and Eastern Europe that are involved in the creation, sale, and distribution of malicious software. This chapter will explore the products and services available in the market, as well as the supply, demand, and price for these resources. In turn, this information will be used to develop estimates for profit margins based on costs and loss metrics for cybercrime campaigns against civilian and business targets.

Data and Methods.

The data for this study came from a sample of 10 publicly accessible web forums; six of these forums trade in bots and other malicious code, while four provide information on programming, malware, and hacking.[29] These data were collected as part of a larger project examining botnets using a snowball sampling procedure in Fall 2007 and Spring 2008.[30] Specifically, two English language forums were identified through *google.com*, using the search term "bot virus carder forum dump." This is a standard technique used by social scientists to collect qualitative data online to obtain a wide sample of prospective sites.[31] After exploring the content of publicly accessible threads from these two sites, six other Russian language forums were identified via web links provided by forum users. In fact, most participants in forums involved in the sale and trade of malware communicate using the Russian language.[32] Thus, a sample of threads from each of these forums was examined by a native-speaking Russian research assistant to ensure the content focused on the sale and exchange of malware. Four additional Russian language forums were identified through links provided in these sites to create this sample of ten forums. Six of these forums focus exclusively on either open sales or requests for malicious software, hacking tools, cybercrime services, and stolen data. The remaining four forums provide a mix of sales, information sharing, and resources to facilitate hacking and malware creation. The names of each forum have been removed to maintain some confidentiality for the participants and forum operators.

Within these 10 forums, all of the available publicly accessible threads were downloaded and saved as web pages. There was a significant volume of information obtained, though the first 50 threads from each forum were translated from Russian to English to assemble a convenient sample of threads. A certified professional translator translated the first 50 threads from eight of the 10 forums. Additionally, 25 threads from Forum 06 and 21 threads from Forum 05 were translated. Due to limited translator availability and duplicate translations in some of the forums, a native Russian graduate student translated additional content.[33] This student translated an additional 150 threads from Forums 03 and 04, and an additional 138 threads from Forum 05. These three forums were selected for further analysis, since they were very active and provided greater detail on the activities and practices of actors within malware markets. Duplicate threads were translated to determine translator reliability, which appeared high across the two translators.

A total of 909 threads derived from this convenient, yet purposeful sample of 10 forums. The threads consisted of 4,049 posts, which provided a copious amount of data to analyze (see Table 2-1 for forum information). Moreover, the forums had a range of user populations, from only 35 to 315 users. These threads span a 4-year period, from 2003 to 2007, though the majority of threads were from 2007.

The translated threads were then printed and analyzed by hand to consider both the prevalence and cost of products and services bought and sold in these forums. A content analysis was conducted to identify products, resources, and materials either sold or sought out in these markets. Advertisement content was coded based on the details provided. A post was coded as a sale if an individual stated that he or she was "selling," "offering," or otherwise providing a service. Requests for products were coded based on the language used, such as "need," "buying," or "seeking." Each item either requested or sold was coded individually, such that an advertisement selling both a piece of malware and a spam database were coded as a single spam database and malware. Thus, the number of advertisements is larger than the overall number of threads where the advertisements appeared.

Forum	Total Number of Strings	Total Number of Posts	User Population	Timeframe Covered
01	50	183	88	6.00 months
02	50	164	50	20.00 months
03	200	1,203	315	10.75 months
04	200	812	273	12.50 months
05	159	369	153	6.75 months
06	50	251	82	36.25 months
07	50	379	116	29.50 months
08	50	291	95	36.00 months
09	50	172	35	10.50 months
10	50	225	95	1.50 months
Total	909	4,049	1,302	

Table 2-1. Descriptive Data on Forums Used.

The threads were also analyzed to determine the services either being sold or requested. Services were coded into categories based on the content of the ad. Specifically, any ad that provided a service, such as the delivery of spam, web hosting, and hacking was coded as "cybercrime services." Ads related to malicious software, including bots, Trojan horses, and iFrame tools, were coded as "malware." Individuals buying or selling credit card account information, records from keystroke logs on compromised machines, or other resources were placed into the category "stolen data." The tag "ICQ numbers" were used for ads selling or requesting ICQ numbers for their personal use. Any advertisement that appeared to be for legitimate products such as computer hardware or software, video game resources, legitimate security or programming services, or other products were placed under the tag "Other Services." Information on stolen data, ICQ numbers, and other services are excluded from this analysis, since they comprise only 36 percent of all threads observed, and are ancillary to malicious software production and services to facilitate cybercrime.[34] Thus, removing these threads enables this analysis to focus on malicious software and cybercrime services in depth.

In order to examine the economics of cybercrime, simple equations and statistics will use data generated from two well known and highly regarded sources: the Computer Security Institute's (CSI) *Annual Computer Crime and Security Survey* and the Internet Crime Complaint Center's (IC3) *Annual Internet Crime Report*. The CSI report is developed in conjunction with the FBI and provides one of the few available resources for statistics on the economic impact of cybercrime in corporate settings. This survey is distributed to 5,000 businesses and organizations across the United States via physical and electronic mail.[35] Two follow-up solicitations are made, and the response rate is usually between 5 and 10 percent of all total recipients. As a result, the figures presented are most likely biased samples that may not accurately reflect the true costs of various attacks across businesses and institutions.

A similar bias is evident in the statistics provided by the Internet Crime Complaint Center. The agency is a joint operation of the FBI and National White Collar Crime Center, which takes reports from individuals who self-identify as victims of certain types of online fraud.[36] Individuals must report any incident via an online form hosted on the IC3 website. Anyone who is not aware of this resource may not report his or her experiences, reducing the generalizability of the data. Additionally, since victims must estimate the loss they have experienced, the reported statistics may not accurately reflect the true costs of victimization.

Despite the validity and generalizability of the statistics produced by these agencies, there are few other consistently reported and widely cited resources on the economic harm caused by cybercrime. Thus, the data produced by these agencies preclude strong conclusions and limit the generalizability of the analysis. The significant lack of research in this area, however, demands that some exploratory investigation be conducted to provide initial estimates for both corporate or individual losses and the general return on investment for cybercrime. The statistics presented are based on the 2008 reports provided by each agency, since they reflect all reported incidents for the 2007 calendar year. This creates a consistent data point between the forum content and the economic harm reported by victims of cybercrime. Since the CSI received a very low response rate in 2008 and did not publish all economic loss estimates, data from the 2007 CSI report[37] will also be used to provide cost measures for certain offenses.

Finally, all the economic data estimated in this analysis do not include labor costs. It is unknown how many man-hours may be required to complete a successful attack due to variations in the actors' skill and technical expertise.[38] Similarly, the time spent to generate new infections or maintain an existing compromise may differ by attacker, based on the sophistication and ease with which they can manage the tools at their disposal.[39] Certain attacks may also require no investment on the part of the offender when paying for a service like a DDoS attack. Thus, time and labor costs will not be included in these economic estimates due to the difficulty in computing these figures.

FINDINGS

Before discussing the products available, it is necessary to consider the structure of the market as a whole. These forums comprise an interconnected marketplace composed of unique threads that act as an advertising space. Individuals created threads by posting their products or services to the rest of the forum. Alternatively, posters could describe in detail what they wanted in buying or acquiring on the open market. Both buyers and sellers provided as thorough a description of their products or tools as possible, including contact information, pricing information, and payment methods. Actors within these markets communicated primarily through the instant messaging protocol ICQ or email, which they can encrypt to protect both participants during the sales process. Some also used the private message (PM) feature built into each forum. PMs ensure quick contact and act as an internal messaging system for each site, though they may not be as secure.

Prices were in either U.S. dollars or Russian rubles, along with the desired method of payment through a web-based electronic payment system. Most participants used WebMoney [WM] or Yandex, since they enable the near-immediate transmission of funds between participants, with no need for face-to-face interactions. In addition, four of the forums identified offered guarantor payment services, in which individuals act as middlemen to hold money on behalf of a buyer until the seller delivers the products or services ordered.[40] Guarantor services ensure a higher likelihood of successful transactions, because both the buyer and seller are aware they can withdraw that payment depending on delivery of an order. Thus, access to a guarantor service is an important way to ensure that transactions are successfully completed in a timely fashion.

There were, however, no actual public transactions of services observed in these forums. Instead, buyers and sellers gave some indication of how the process operated. An interested individual would contact the advertiser via ICQ or email and negotiate the cost for services rendered. The prospective buyer then pays for the product and awaits delivery from the seller. Many sellers indicated that they must receive payment in advance of services rendered. This process introduces the potential for buyers to lose money should a good or service fail to be provided, and facilitates buyers being cheated by untrustworthy operatives. As a result, the sales process appears to favor sellers rather than buyers.

Malware.

The most common resource available in malicious software markets were Trojan horse programs (see Table 2-2 for breakdown).[41] There were 78 ads related to Trojan horse programs, comprising 31.7 percent of all malware for sale. The cost of these programs varied significantly, from $2 to $5,000, depending on the quality and sophistication of the resource. A variety of Trojan horses were sold, ranging from well-known resources like Pinch, which can steal information from over 30 well-known programs, to keylogging Trojan horses designed to steal funds from WebMoney accounts. There was a relative balance between sale ads (51.6 percent) and custom request ads (49.4 percent) seeking Trojan horse programs. Thus, there is still a significant demand for novel or unique Trojan horses with special qualities that may not otherwise sell on the open market.

The second most common malware were iFrame tools that enable the distribution and infection by unique malicious code through web browsers (30.5 percent). The concept and design of iFrames originate with .html programming to seamlessly push multiple .html files to a browser in a single page of content without the need for user interaction.[42] Hackers subverted this design function, however, to surreptitiously send malware to unsuspecting users. In fact, individuals sold iFrame "exploits" and "packs" one could place on a server to infect the personal computers of individuals who visit web pages hosted there. This type of attack exponentially increases the infection vector for malicious software, and the risk of identity theft, data loss, and computer misuse.[43] There were 14 ads (66 percent) selling access to iFrame scripts and infection packs, indicating there is a healthy supply of these tools on the market. The proportion of requests for these resources (34 percent) also suggests there is still a substantial demand for iFrame malware. The price for these products ranged from $2 to $450, depending on the quality and sophistication of the resource. This is somewhat lower than the prices for Trojan horses, potentially because of the unique application of iFrame tools and the knowledge required to establish the infrastructure and support infections.

Resources Max.	Number of Average	Percent of		Buy	Percent of	Sell	Percent of		Min
	Posts	Total	Posts	Total	Posts	Total	Price	Price	Price
Bots	16	6.5	8	50	8	50	30	2,000	322.27
Bugs	3	1.2	3	100	0	0	40	40	40.00
Cryptors, Joiners, and Polymorphic Engines	47	19.1	13	27.6	34	72.4	0.20	49	13.03
FTP Resources	27	11.0	15	55.6	12	44.4	20	1,000	271.66
iFrames and Traffic Sales	75	30.5	26	34.7	49	65.3			
Tools	21	28.0	7	33.3	14	66.6	2	450	79.25
Traffic	54	72.0	19	35.2	35	64.8	1	500	110.84
Trojan horses	78	31.7	38	48.7	40	51.3	2	5,000	742.97
Total	246	100	103	41.9	143	58.1			

**Table 2-2. Malware and Related Services Offered
in Hacker Forums.**

In addition, 72 percent of all iFrame ads involved hackers leasing access to their active iFrame infrastructure on compromised servers through "traffic streams." Selling traffic enabled individuals to make a profit by uploading someone else's malware to the server so that it could be used to infect individual users. There were a number of iFrame traffic sellers, and their ads comprised 64.8 percent of the traffic market, suggesting that there may be some saturation of this resource in the hacker community. Most traffic stream providers based their pricing on 1,000 infections, with an average cost of $110.84 per 1,000 systems. Sellers also explained that they could acquire infections in specific countries, and streams in the United States tended to have the highest price overall. Mixed traffic from various countries around the world was sold at the lowest overall price.

The third most prevalent form of malware sold were programs designed to either conceal or encrypt malicious code so it could be sent and activated undetected by antivirus programs. These tools were largely referred to as cryptors, and comprised 19.1 percent of the total programs offered in the malware market. Most individuals sold cryptors (72.4 percent), suggesting that these tools are readily available across the market. The average price for a cryptor was $13.03, which is substantially lower than all other forms of malware. This may stem from the utility of cryptor software, since it is not necessary to facilitate an attack. Thus, individuals may be more likely to sell these programs at a lower price in order to attract prospective customers.

Hackers also offered compromised File Transfer Protocol (FTP) servers, which hold sensitive information including web page content, databases, email accounts, and other data. FTP resources comprised 11 percent of the overall malware market, and the price depended on the quality and quantity of data offered. The average cost of FTP resources was $271.66 per item, and there was a substantial demand for these services. In fact, 55 percent of the ads involved requests for specific servers or attacks. Thus, individuals could seek out someone to complete an attack on their behalf as a service, rather than take the time to complete this act on their own.

The final types of malware offered in the markets were bots, which constitute 6.5 percent of all malware bought and sold. Eight individuals offered either unique executables of bot programs or leased their existing infrastructure for spam distribution or as an attack platform. There was an equal demand for custom builds of bot malware, suggesting there was a strong demand to create and establish individual botnets. The average cost of bot services was also higher than that of iFrame resources at $322.27, but lower than the price of a Trojan horse. The generally small proportion of ads related to bot malware may stem from the sizeable proportion of botnet-driven services available in the market.

Cybercrime Services.

A diverse range of products enabling individuals to engage in a variety of cybercrimes was also available in the market, including Distributed Denial of Service (DDoS) attacks, spam, attacks, and hosting malicious content online (Table 2-3). The primary service offered in these forums related to the distribution of spam (32.4 percent), or unwanted messages to email accounts, ICQ numbers, and mobile phones. The largest subcategory related to spam involved email databases that could be used to create distribution lists for spam delivery. Database sales and requests comprised 46.5 percent of the overall spam threads. Twenty-four individuals across five of the sites sold databases for spam, with variable costs based on the number of emails and the country location for each address. The majority of these ads involved sales of existing databases (78.8 percent), suggesting that there is a substantial supply of email addresses in the marketplace.

Resources	Number Percent of Posts Total	Percent of Min. Total Price	Buy Max. Posts Price	Percent of Average Total Price	Sell post
DDoS*	29	13.01	0	0.0	29
	100.0	0.41	25	14.26	
Hacking Services 47.7	30	14.0	16	53.3	14
Compromise 45.5	11	36.7	6	54.5	5
Email/Passwords 47.4	19	63.3	10	52.6	9
Proxies and VPN 84.0	25	11.4	4	16.0	21
Proxy 80.0	20	80.0	4	20.0	16
VPN 100.0	5	20.0	0	0.0	5
Spam Services 80.3	71	32.4	14	19.7	57
Databases	33	46.5	7	21.2	26
78.80.50	100	45.43			
Services	23	32.4	3	13.0	20
87.00.50	700	50.91			
Tools	15	21.1	4	26.7	11
73.32.00	180	59.11			
Web Hosting and Services 90.6	64	29.2	6	9.4	58
Domains 91.7	24	37.5	2	8.3	22
Hosting	30	46.9	3	10.0	27
90.00.853.00	48.89				
Registration	10	15.6	1	10.0	9
90.09.00	150	50.17			
Total 82.2	219	100.0	39	17.8	180

* Due to variation in pricing, DDoS estimates are based on the stated hourly rate or an average hourly rate based on prices for 24-hour attack.

Table 2-3: Cybercrime Services Offered in Hacker Forums.[#]

[#]Due to significant missing data, hacking services, domain sales, and VPN service pricing are not included here.

The second largest subcategory of spam involved ads related to the actual distribution of spam messages. The majority of these ads were sales-related (87 percent), suggesting that there was significant market saturation for this service. In addition, the price for spam distribution was generally low, with an average of $50.91. Sellers often described giving substantial discounts for sizeable deliveries, with the final cost for spam distribution at an average of less than .0001 cent per message. Thus, the distribution of spam is a relatively inexpensive service to acquire. Finally, there were 18 threads (21.1 percent) pertaining to scripts and mailing programs to facilitate the distribution of spam. The average price for spam tools was $59.11, which was the most expensive average price in this category. The proliferation of spam resources suggests that this is now a service-driven product for attackers, requiring minimal knowledge of computer systems and networks.

Individuals also offered services to support a variety of malicious web content. Hackers need resources to host malicious content, such as malware or cracked software; thus, web hosting and domain resources comprised 29.2 percent of the threads related to cyber-crime services in these markets. There were 30 threads related to web hosting made by 22 different user-names in five forums. Additionally, there were only three requests (10 percent) for web hosting services, suggesting there is a substantial supply of providers available. Descriptions of the hosting services varied, depending on the amount of storage needed and their desired level of customer support. The price range for service was variable, ranging from 50 cents to $300, with an average of $48.89. Thus, hosting services could be obtained for a generally low price, depending on individual needs.

Sellers also indicated what content they would not host in their ads. In particular, child pornography and bestiality-related content were regularly viewed as unacceptable. Hosting this sort of content may pose too much risk for a provider, since many countries have legislation and law enforcement initiatives to combat child pornography.[44] By contrast, malware was often cited as acceptable demonstrating the key intersection between malware and cybercrime service providers.

There were also nine individuals offering domain name registration services in order to shield actor identities from law enforcement and domain registration authorities. Since 90 percent of these ads were sales-related, there is a clear supply of providers within the market. In addition, seven individuals sold web domains comprising 37.5 percent of these services. Thus, there appears to be a solid support infrastructure in place to aid hackers in developing, hosting, and maintaining malicious web content.

Hacking services comprised 14 percent of all service-related posts, and offered two primary forms of attack. The first was account-related, including obtaining passwords from email accounts, website log-in screens, and forums in a surreptitious fashion. Eleven ads appeared in this sample of threads, suggesting that there is a relatively high demand (45.5 percent) for assistance with hacking. The second form involved compromising or attacking a specific target. There were 19 requests for compromise assistance with a similar distribution of buyers (52.6 percent) to sellers (47.4 percent). Specifically, 10 individuals requested assistance in obtaining access to different systems, ranging from hacking FTP servers to acquiring spam databases from specific websites. Nine users also advertised hacking services to order, including attacking Google Page Ranking systems or acquiring passwords for email accounts. These ads did not provide any substantive information on pricing, making it difficult to determine price metrics. At the same time, the prevalence of requests and available service providers demonstrates that these forums engender individuals to engage in forms of cybercrime that may exceed their technical capabilities.

A proportion of sellers also offered DDoS attack services for a fee. These services comprised 13 percent of the overall posts related to cybercrime services in these forums including 29 ads across four of the forums (see Table 2-3 for detail). Sellers offered to flood a web server with requests, rendering them unable to complete the information exchange necessary to fulfill user requests for content.[45] As a result, individuals are unable to access resources hosted on the server for the duration of the attack. DDoS providers regularly mentioned that their services were supported by botnets, as in an ad from one provider who noted "Large quantity of BOTS online, quantity grows every day. BOTs are located in different time belts [zones], which allows the DDoS to work 24 hours a day." All of the ads in this sample were sales-related, indicating that these providers have completely saturated the market and are readily accessible to interested parties. The average cost for DDoS services was $14.26 per hour, indicating that this service is also relatively inexpensive.

The final service identified in these forums offered access to proxy services and Virtual Private Networks (VPN). These resources conceal an individual's IP address and location, reducing the likelihood of detection while one is engaging in attacks or malicious activity online by routing packet traffic from the user's system through IP addresses on a server.[46] The majority of ads for both proxy and VPN services were sales-related (84 percent), suggesting there is a significant supply of these services within the malware market. The pricing for proxy services were often tiered based on the total number of proxies purchased, though the average cost of proxy services was $42.52. There was, however, too much missing data to calculate the cost of VPN services. Nevertheless, these findings suggest that tools to conceal an actor's location were readily accessible through these forums.

Examining the Economics of Cybercrime.

The cost metrics derived from these forums makes it possible to consider the economic gains individuals may generate from the use of malware and cybercrime services. For instance, the significant number of Trojan horses advertised calls into question the costs and benefits of obtaining malware for attack purposes. Using the average costs for tools, it is possible that an attacker may spend $755.80 to acquire a Trojan horse ($742.77) and encryption software ($13.03) to increase the likelihood of infection. If the attacker were to attempt to target victims randomly in order to establish an infection, he or she may distribute infected files via spam email.[47] If a proportion of unsuspecting recipients open the file, this may immediately create a series of infections with minimal effort. The average cost to obtain an email address from an existing database or send a message is .0001 cents. Thus, it would cost approximately .0002 cents to obtain and send a message to a single email address using the providers identified in these forums. At this rate, an individual would spend $20 to send out 100,000 spam messages. Adding this figure to the software costs increases the overall offender investment for a malware campaign to $775.80.

Comparing this figure against the loss to business and industry indicates that there is a significant difference in the harm that a hacker can cause. The CSI report indicates that the cost of remediating a virus or worm infection is $40,141 per respondent.[48] Thus, the cost to a victimized business can be up to 53 times greater than the initial investment made by the offender. Simple destruction or infections do not, however, generate revenue for an attacker. Instead, they must obtain sensitive data through key-loggers or mass intrusions into database information. These losses can be exponentially worse, as the average cost for the theft of proprietary data was $241,000 per respondent, and $268,000 for stolen customer or employee data.[49] Thus, the profit margin for malware acquisition can be substantial, depending on the quality and quantity of data acquired.

Examining the cost of botnet establishment and mitigation reveals a similarly high profit margin. For example, if an individual pays the average cost of $322.27 to acquire botnet software, and an additional $200 to send out a million spam messages, his or her total investment is $522.27. Within corporate environments, the average cost to mitigate and remove a botnet infection was $345,600 per respondent.[50] Using this metric, if a bot herder were able to establish 10 nodes across five companies, it is feasible that this might cause over $1.7 million dollars in damages. In addition, he or she could regain the initial investment costs by leasing their bot infrastructure to engage in a single 37-hour DDoS attack if he or she charged the average rate of $14.26 per hour. Alternatively, the bot herder would need to send out at least 5.2 million spam messages through his or her infrastructure at .0001 cents per message to earn back the investment.

A similar rate of return can be found with iFrame campaigns. If an offender wanted to establish his or her own iFrame service over a 6-month period, the offender may have to acquire three resources. First, the offender may spend up to $450 to purchase the most expensive iFrame kit available in the market. Second, if the offender does not have the capacity to compromise and install the kit on a server, he or she may identify a third-party web-hosting service for the kit. In this scenario, the offender would pay an average of $48.89 to host the malware each month for a total of $293.34. In addition, a weekly spam campaign may prove useful in order to drive prospective victims to the website. In this scenario, the individual would have to spend $4,800 to send out one million spam messages each week at $200 over a 24-week period. In total, an offender using each of these services, including paying the maximum for an iFrame kit, would spend $5,543.34 over a 6-month period.

If the attacker is successful and generating traffic, he or she may choose to lease out the infrastructure to generate a profit. Using the average cost metric for traffic sales at $110.84 per 1,000 infections, the offender would need to generate consistent traffic and infect at least 50,000 systems from mixed traffic to regain his or her initial investment. It is unclear from the posts and comments from sellers how long it takes to generate such traffic, though the sheer number of traffic resellers suggests that it is possible to establish and maintain such an infrastructure over time. Thus, there appears to be some substantial return on investment for iFrame operators who are willing to make operational expenditures in their infrastructure over time.

Since malware requires time, money, and some skill to use properly, some offenders may opt to lease services from providers in the market. For instance, the availability of DDoS services in the forum suggests that individuals may be interested in paying for an attack rather than creating and maintaining their own botnet. Since the average cost of DDoS services in these forums was $14.26 per hour, a botmaster may generate an estimated $342.24 per day for a 24-hour attack. It is also clear that lengthy attacks decrease productivity and increase financial harm for the target. Thus, an offender may spend $1,026.72 for a 3-day attack based on a 72-hour rate at $14.26 per hour. This is most likely an overestimate, as DDoS providers offered discounted prices based on the length of an attack. Regardless, victims lost an average of $14,889.69 from DDoS attacks in 2006.[51] This is a substantial impact that well exceeds the initial cost paid by the offender.

A successful DDoS attack does not, however, generate any observable economic gain for the individual who ordered the attack. As a consequence, it is necessary to consider how an individual may use a DDoS provider to generate a substantial profit. To that end, a number of hackers blackmail businesses by threatening to take their systems offline using DDoS attacks. Prospective targets often pay ransoms to avoid a loss of service or embarrassment over a prospective attack.[52] In fact, CSI respondents paid an average of $824.74 to avoid or stop attacks in 2006.[53] To that end, a botmaster or his or her prospective client could readily generate a profit by simply threatening to attack a company. It is unclear how long an attack would need to take place to ensure payment of a ransom, though if an offender had to pay for a 24- to 48-hour attack, he or she could still generate a profit of approximately $150 or more based on the average business cost. The profit margin increases substantially if an attack ends within a matter of hours. Thus, blackmail may be an extremely useful way to utilize DDoS services.

The same profit margins are evident in the use of spam providers. Since an individual attacker may spend approximately .0002 cents to obtain and send a message to a single email address, his initial investment is quite small. The likelihood of successful responses is equally low, since there are myriad security tools designed to filter or block spam messages from reaching the end user.[54] Depending on the scheme employed, however, an attacker need only affect a small number of users in order to make a profit. For instance, advance fee fraud ("419 scams") is one of the most economically rewarding spam schemes.[55] In these frauds, the sender poses as a banker, barrister, or wealthy heiress seeking assistance to move a large sum of money out of the country. The senders say they need the assistance of a trustworthy foreigner to help them complete this transaction due to various legal or familial issues. All that the victim needs to do is provide his or her name, address, and banking information, and in return that person can retain a portion of the total dollar amount described.[56]

Though it is unknown how many individuals who receive these messages actually respond to the fraudulent solicitation, estimates state that between 1 and 3 percent of all recipients are victims.[57] In addition, data from the Internet Crime Complaint Center suggest that victims lose an average of $1,922.99 when participating in the scheme.[58] With this in mind, if an offender spends $200 to send out one million advance fee fraud messages, he may receive an overly conservative response rate of .00005, or 50 recipients. Using the IC3 average dollar loss for this sort of scam, a cybercriminal could earn $96,149.50 from these 50 respondents, which is 480 times their initial investment. Though these scams require a significant degree of human interaction with the victim and labor in order to be successful, the profit margin is still exceedingly high. Thus, spam distribution services are a key resource in the larger marketplace for cybercrime, and its low price may reflect the difficulty in effectively targeting and ensuring a high rate of return from an investment.

DISCUSSION AND CONCLUSIONS

This monograph sought to explore the market for malicious software and cybercrime services in order to understand the price and availability of resources, as well as the relationship between the price paid for services and the cost experienced by victims of these crimes. The findings suggest that myriad tools and services are available and sold for profit in an open market environment that encourages and supports cybercrime.[59] Individuals could procure spam, DDoS attack services, Trojan horses, iFrame exploit infections, web hosting, and various other resources at relatively low prices from the forums in this sample. Several of these services also depend on botnets for functionality, demonstrating the prominence of this malware in cybercrime.

The pricing structure and observed supply and demand for different resources suggest that these markets have made it easier for individuals to engage in computer intrusions and attacks. Participants in these forums no longer need to cultivate high levels of skill and technological sophistication, since they could readily request assistance to compromise email accounts or servers, and lease existing infrastructure created by more skilled actors.[60] In fact, botmasters appear to recognize the value of their infrastructure and offer services enabled by their infrastructure to generate a profit. In turn, the marketplace appears to operate largely as a service economy in which individuals can select from multiple providers based on price and customer service in order to complete an attack that may well exceed their overall level of knowledge.

Examining the return on investment for engaging in various cybercrime schemes also suggests that attackers can generate a substantial profit or cause damage that far exceeds their initial investment. In fact, some of the least expensive products, such as spam distribution, may provide a massive gain for the individual attacker and a slight profit for the service provider. In addition, individuals who own and operate bot and iFrame infrastructure may generate a substantial profit over time by leasing their services. Those who lease or pay fees for service may, however, have a reduced risk of detection from law enforcement because they do not actually compromise systems or have a significant relationship to the affected systems. In addition, their profit margins may be slightly higher due to minimal labor and maintenance costs. Their limited skill set may diminish their overall earning lifetime capacity, since they may never cultivate the necessary skills to create and complete their own intrusions and attacks.

The findings of this exploratory analysis must be interpreted with caution due to the inherent limitations of the data. Specifically, the victimization statistics used in this analysis have extremely limited generalizability and are most likely biased samples representing small proportions of the total population. In addition, the CSI reports indicate that less than a third of all incidents that occur are reported to law enforcement.[61] Thus, there is a critical need for increased reporting of cybercrime and improved measures for corporate and individual losses. The paucity of data in this area makes it difficult to understand or estimate the efficacy of cyber attacks and the overall economic gains made by offenders. Increased clarity in reporting is vital to move criminological and information security research beyond speculation, and to move case studies into quantifiable areas of loss calculation. In turn, one can better understand the economics of both attack and defense.

Additionally, the data used for the forum analyses derive from publicly accessible forums that are over 3 years old. The content of the data may be radically different from the resources available in private forums, which require registration and membership vetting in order to access posts.[62] In addition, the rapid changes in technology make it difficult to extrapolate these findings to the current resources that may be available in the malware marketplace. Finally, this analysis used a small proportion of threads from multiple forums, which may limit the amount of malware and services observed. Thus, there is a need for greater research to understand the practices and content of malware markets over time. Longitudinal research can provide insights into the shifts in available resources, and identify any declines or spikes in the price for a good or service. Such research can also identify new trends in malware and attack vectors, improving the response capabilities of law enforcement and security professionals. Future research should also develop comparative samples of threads from open and closed forums to consider variations in the products that can be acquired by those with greater penetration into and status in the hacker community. In turn, this can substantially improve our understanding of the skill and ability present in the hacker community and its operational capabilities.

ENDNOTES - CHAPTER 2

1. S. Furnell, *Cybercrime: Vandalizing the Information Society,* Boston, MA: Addison-Wesley, 2002; Y. Jewkes and K. Sharp, "Crime, Deviance and the Disembodied Self: Transcending the Dangers of Corporeality" in Y. Jewkes, ed., *Dot.cons: Crime, Deviance and Identity on the Internet,* Portland, OR: Willan Publishing, 2003, pp. 1-14; D. S. Wall, *Cybercrime: The Transformation of Crime in the Information Age,* Cambridge, UK: Polity Press, 2007.

2. S. W. Brenner, *Cyberthreats: The Emerging Fault Lines of the Nation State,* New York: Oxford University Press, 2008; D. E. Denning, "Activism, Hacktivism, and Cyberterrorism: The Internet as a Tool for Influencing Foreign Policy," J. Arquilla and D. F. Ronfeldt, eds., *Networks and Netwars: The Future of Terror, Crime, and Militancy,* Santa Monica, CA: Rand, 2001; T. J. Holt and E. Lampke, "Exploring Stolen Data Markets On-Line: Products and Market Forces," *Criminal Justice Studies,* Vol. 23, 2010, pp. 33-50; The Honeynet Project, *Know Your Enemy: Learning About Security Threats,* Boston, MA: Addison-Wesley, 2001.

3. T. J. Holt, "Examining a Transnational Problem: An Analysis of Computer Crime Victimization in Eight Countries from 1999 to 2001," *International Journal of Comparative and Applied Criminal Justice,* Vol. 27, 2003, pp. 199-220.

4. Brenner, *Cyberthreats;* Denning, "Activism, Hactivism, and Cyberterrorism"; T. J. Holt, J. B. Soles, and L. Leslie, "Characterizing Malware Writers and Computer Attackers in Their Own Words," paper presented at the International Conference on Information Warfare and Security, Peter Kiewit Institute, University of Nebraska Omaha, NE, 2008.

5. *Ibid.*

6. Brenner, Cyberthreats; Denning, "Activism, Hactivism, and Cyberterrorism"; E. V. Kapersky, *The Classification of Computer Viruses*, Bern, Switzerland: Metropolitan Network BBS Inc., 2003, available from *www.avp.ch/avpve/classes/classes.stm*; P. Szor, *The Art of Computer Virus Research and Defense*, Upper Saddle River, NJ: Addison-Wesley, 2005; R. W. Taylor, E. J. Fritsch, J. Liederbach, and T. J. Holt, *Digital Crime and Digital Terrorism*, 2nd Ed., Upper Saddle River, NJ: Pearson Prentice Hall, 2010.

7. Taylor *et al.*, *Digital Crime and Digital Terrorism.*

8. B. Chu, T. J. Holt, and G. J Ahn, *Examining the Creation, Distribution, and Function of Malware On-Line,"* Washington, DC, National Institute of Justice, 2010, available from *www.ncjrs.gov./pdffiles1/nij/grants/230112.pdf*; J. Franklin, V. Paxson, A Perrig, and S. Savage, "An Inquiry Into the Nature and Cause of the Wealth of Internet Miscreants,"paper presented at CCS07, October 29-November 2007; T. J. Holt and E. Lampke, "Exploring Stolen Data Markets On-Line: Products and Market Forces," *Criminal Justice Studies*, Vol. 23, 2010, pp. 33-50; Honeynet Research Alliance, *Profile: Automated Credit Card Fraud*, 2003, available from *www.honeynet.org/papers/profiles/cc-fraud.pdf*; R. Thomas and J. Martin. 2006. "The Underground Economy: Priceless," *:login* Vol. 31, 2003, pp. 7-16.

9. *Ibid.*

10. T. J. Holt and M. Kilger, "Techcrafters and Makecrafters: A Comparison of Two Populations of Hackers," *2008 WOMBAT Workshop on Information Security Threats Data Collection and Sharing*, 2008, pp. 67-78

11. Furnell, *Cybercrime*; T. J. Holt, "Subcultural Evolution? Examining the Influences of On- and Off-Line Experiences on Deviant Subcultures," *Deviant Behavior*, Vol. 28, 2007, pp. 171-198; Holt *et al.*, "Characterizing Malware Writers"; T. Jordan and P. A. Taylor, "A Sociology of Hackers," *The Sociological Review*, Vol. 46, 1998, pp. 757-780; P. A. Taylor, *Hackers: Crime in the Digital Sublime*, New York: Routledge, 1999.

12. *Ibid.*

13. Holt, "Subcultural Evolution?"; Holt and Kilger, "Techcrafters and Makecrafters"; The Honeynet Project, *Know Your Enemy*; Jordan and Taylor, "A Sociology of Hackers."

14. *Ibid.*

15. Holt, "Subcultural Evolution?"; T. J. Holt and M. Kilger, "Techcrafters and Makecrafters"; Holt *et al.*, "Characterizing Malware Writers"; The Honeynet Project, *Know Your Enemy*; Jordan and Taylor, "A Sociology of Hackers."

16. The Honeynet Project, *Know Your Enemy*; G. R. Meyer, *The Social Organization of the Computer Underground,* Unpublished Masters Thesis, 1989, available from *www.csrc.nist.gov/secpubs/hacker.txt*; Taylor, *Hackers.*

17. Franklin *et al.*, "An Inquiry Into the Nature and Cause of the Wealth of Internet Miscreants"; Holt and Lampke, "Exploring Stolen Data Markets On-Line"; Honeynet Research Alliance, *Profile: Automated Credit Card Fraud,* 2003; Thomas and Martin, "The Underground Economy: Priceless."

18. *Ibid.*

19. *Ibid.*

20. Chu *et al.*, *Examining the Creation, Distribution, and Function of Malware On-line* ; Franklin *et al.*, "An Inquiry Into the Nature and Cause of the Wealth of Internet Miscreants"; Honeynet Research Alliance, *Profile: Automated Credit Card Fraud,* 2003; Thomas and Martin, "The Underground Economy: Priceless."

21. Brenner, *Cyberthreats*; Furnell, *Cybercrime*; Holt, "Examining at Transnational Problem"; H. Stambaugh, D. S. Beaupre, D. J. Icove, R. Baker, W. Cassady, and W. P. Williams, *Electronic Crime Needs Assessment for State and Local Law Enforcement,* Washington, DC: National Institute of Justice; Taylor *et al.*, *Digital Crime and Digital Terrorism.Wall, Cybercrime.*

22. *Ibid.*

23. Taylor *et al.*, *Digital Crime and Digital Terrorism.*

24. Holt, "Examining at Transnational Problem"; Taylor *et al.*, *Digital Crime and Digital Terrorism.*

25. *Ibid.*

26. Computer Security Institute, *Computer Crime and Security Survey*, 2008, available from *www.cybercrime.gov/FBI2008.pdf.*

27. *Ibid.*

28. Internet Crime Complaint Center, *IC3 2008 Internet Crime Report*, available from *www.ic3.gov/media/annualreport/2008_IC3Report.pdf.*

29. See Chu *et al.*, *Examining the Creation, Distribution, and Function of Malware On-line* for additional detail.

30. *Ibid.*

31. C. Hine, ed., *Virtual Methods: Issues in Social Research on the Internet,* Oxford, UK: Berg, 2005; T. J. Holt, "Exploring Strategies for Qualitative Criminological and Criminal Justice Inquiry Using On-Line Data," *Journal of Criminal Justice Education,* Vol. 21, 2010, pp. 466-487.

32. Thomas and Martin, "The Underground Economy: Priceless."

33. The graduate translator provided translations from seven forums: six threads from forum 02; 150 from forums 03 and 04; 138 from forum 05; 25 from forum 06; one from forum 07; and one from forum 09.

34. See Chu *et al.*, *Examining the Creation, Distribution, and Function of Malware On-line* for additional detail.

35. Computer Security Institute, *Computer Crime and Security Survey*, 2008.

36. Internet Crime Complaint Center, *IC3 2008 Internet Crime Report.*

37. Computer Security Institute, *Computer Crime and Security Survey,* 2007, available from *www.cybercrime.gov/FBI2007.pdf.*

38. S. Gordon, *Virus and Vulnerability Classification Schemes: Standards and Integration,* Symantec Security Response, 2003, available from *enterprisesecurity.symantec.com/content/knowledgeli-brary.cfm?EID=0*; Holt *et al.,* "Characterizing Malware Writers"; The Honeynet Project, *Know Your Enemy;* Jordan and Taylor, "A Sociology of Hackers."

39. *Ibid.*

40. *Ibid.*

41. It must be noted that two individuals sought out individuals who could identify zero-day vulnerabilities in systems so that they could be exploited for an attack. A third individual was selling information about a bug within the market. These posts, however, comprise only 1.2 percent of all malware-related posts, and are not discussed in detail in the larger text.

42. N. Provos, P. Mavrommatis, M. A. Rajab, and F. Monrose, "All Your iFRAMEs Point to Us," *Proceedings of the 17th Conference on Security Symposium*, 2008, pp. 1-15.

43. Provos *et al.,* "All Your iFRAMEs Point to Us."

44. Taylor *et al., Digital Crime and Digital Terrorism.*

45. Brenner, *Cyberthreats;* Taylor *et al., Digital Crime and Digital Terrorism;* Wall, *Cybercrime.*

46. *Ibid.*

47. *Ibid.*

48. Computer Security Institute, *Computer Crime and Security Survey,* 2008.

49. *Ibid.*

50. *Ibid.*

51. Since these data are not available in the 2008 report, this statistic is derived from the Computer Security Institute, *Computer Crime and Security Survey*, 2007.

52. Brenner, *Cyberthreats;* Taylor *et al.*, *Digital Crime and Digital Terrorism.*

53. Computer Security Institute, *Computer Crime and Security Survey*, 2007.

54. T. J. Holt and D. C. Graves. "A Qualitative Analysis of Advanced Fee Fraud Schemes," *The International Journal of Cyber-Criminology* Vol. 1, 2007, pp. 137-154.

55. Holt and Graves, "A Qualitative Analysis"; Taylor *et al.*, *Digital Crime and Digital Terrorism.*

56. *Ibid.*

57. *Ibid.*

58. Internet Crime Complaint Center. *IC3 2008 Internet Crime Report.*

59. Franklin *et al.*, "An Inquiry Into the Nature and Cause of the Wealth of Internet Miscreants"; Holt and Lampke, "Exploring Stolen Data Markets On-Line"; Honeynet Research Alliance, *Profile: Automated Credit Card Fraud*, 2003; Thomas and Martin, "The Underground Economy: Priceless."

60. Holt and Kilger, "Techcrafters and Makecrafters"; Jordan and Taylor, "A Sociology of Hackers."

61. Computer Security Institute, *Computer Crime and Security Survey*, 2007.

62. Holt, "Exploring Strategies for Qualitative Criminological and Criminal Justice Inquiry Using On-line Data."

CHAPTER 3

THE EMERGENCE OF THE
CIVILIAN CYBER WARRIOR

Max Kilger

Note: The information in the chapter derives from a current study by the author and other researchers.

INTRODUCTION

The advantages gained from making a concerted effort to develop an understanding of an adversary are difficult to overstate. Whether the analysis occurs through a psychological, social-psychological, anthropological, or strictly sociological perspective, the ability to "know your enemy" is a critical component of a comprehensive strategy to protect assets actively and proactively within critical infrastructures. While the deployment of defensive technical barriers, such as firewalls, intrusion detection systems, etc., are necessary actions to provide sufficient protection for digital networks that hold sensitive data or have supervisory control and data acquisition (SCADA) functions, the ability to develop a taxonomy of the perpetrators' motivations behind the vectors within the cyber-threat matrix can assist in making a more accurate assessment of the threat each type of actor presents to specific elements within specific infrastructures. In addition, developing a foundational understanding of the motivations of malicious online actors facilitates the ability to construct plausible future threat scenarios that may emerge in the near- to mid-term timeline.

This chapter will start by providing some basic background for a schema that outlines six hypothesized motivational factors to encourage malicious online behaviors. The focus of the discussion will then turn to one specific motivation and within that motivation, one specific archetype—the civilian cyber warrior—that poses perhaps the most significant emerging threat to domestic and foreign critical infrastructures. Finally, the chapter will conclude with an analysis of some preliminary data in an ongoing study that investigates some of the factors that may relate to this specific type of online malicious actor.

THEORETICAL BACKGROUND

Over the years, there have been a number of attempts to create taxonomies for malicious online actors. Many of these taxonomies rely partially upon the factor of skill and expertise possessed by the actor in various operating system platforms, networking protocols, digital hardware functionality, programming languages or shell scripting, or knowledge of specific system security strategies. These taxonomies also to some extent rely upon the type of target that the malicious actor specializes in. The Chiesa study utilized a combination of skill and target type as well as motivational attributes such as political reasons, escape from family situations, and conflict with authority as taxonomy criteria for classifying malicious online actors.[1] The Rogers study described two different dimensions—skill level and motivation—to build a multiclass taxonomy of hackers. His hacker class taxonomy includes classes of hackers such as petty thieves, old guard hackers, professional criminals and, more recently, political activists.[2] In *Cyber Adversary Charac-*

terization: Auditing the Hacker Mind, Tom Parker, Eric Shaw, Ed Stroz, Mathew Devost, and Marcus Sachs place emphasis not only on the properties of the attacker, but their model also examines in detail other factors such as the perceived probability of success of attack, perceived probability of detection and, other attack-associated metrics.[3]

The classification schema in this chapter is one developed by this author, Ofir Arkman, and Jeff Stutzman.[4] This schema—labeled MEECES[5]—describes six motivations for malicious online actors: Money, Ego, Entrance to social group, Cause, Entertainment, and Status. Money, of course, is the most obvious and self- explanatory motivation. The significant extent to which financial institutions have placed financial resources, such as checking, savings, credit lines, credit cards, and other components of the banking system online, has put tremendous amounts of financial capital at potential risk. The vast potential for wealth that has been exposed to the Internet has attracted a plethora of malicious actors from a number of different backgrounds. In addition to the malicious actors who were already motivated by financial gain, the magnitude of the financial resources available has likely also tempted other skilled individuals who might otherwise not have been spurred to action by this motivation.

Further, there are geo-economic factors at work here as well. Perhaps for the first time, individuals in countries where the standard of living is lower in comparison to first-world industrialized countries, the potential for finding gainful employment is uncertain, and, in some cases, the economic climate has forced highly educated individuals into underemployment, the allure of the possibility of gaining access to and illegally acquiring significant sums of money is great. This has also led to the migration of more traditional organized crime members into the cyber environment. This infusion of sometimes technically unsophisticated criminals into cybercrime has also changed the dynamics of cybercrime gangs.

This was not always the case. During the early years of the hacking community, individuals who used their technical skills for personal monetary gain were shunned by the rest of the community. It was considered a violation of the code of ethics for hackers to deploy their skills to steal money or financial resources. This norm violation is still in place today in the hacking community, but it has been substantially weakened by the increasing number of skilled individuals who utilize their expertise for unlawful financial gain as well as the influx of a more traditional criminal element.

Ego is the second motivation in the schema.[6] Ego motivates individuals through the feelings of accomplishment that accompany overcoming a particularly difficult technical obstacle. Actions such as getting a hardware device to do something that was thought impossible, writing a complicated piece of code that intelligently adapts to situations, or bypassing a sophisticated security system such as a firewall or intrusion detection system are all examples of behaviors associated with the ego motivation. Note that the actions do not necessarily have to be malicious in nature — even difficult obstacles that are overcome in the course of lawful employment relate to this motivation.

The third motivation for malicious online acts is entrance to a social group. Hacking groups are more or less status-homogenous in terms of technical expertise.[7] While there is likely a leader of the hacking group who possesses somewhat higher levels of skill and expertise, the majority of the individual group members have somewhat similar levels of technical proficiency, although it is likely that individuals are proficient in different areas, such as different operating systems or programming languages. This means that in order for an individual to join the group, that individual must possess levels of expertise similar to the members of the group he or she wishes to join. The key question is, how do prospective candidates demonstrate their level of expertise? It is almost certain that the members of the hacking group will not consider the word of the candidate at face value. One of the pathways in which the prospects can demonstrate their skills is writing an elegant piece of malicious code. Once written, the code goes to the hacking group, which in turn evaluates its function and programming aesthetic. If the group feels the code displays at least the minimum skill level necessary to belong to the group, it will admit the candidate. The code itself is often given to the members of the group as a sort of "initiation fee."

Cause is the fourth motivation for malicious online actors. Cause is defined as the use of technical expertise or skill in the pursuit of political, social, cultural, ideological, religious, or nationalistic goals.[8] Hacktivism is one of the more common types of malicious online behavior. The most common hacktivism events often take the form of website defacements. Examples of hacktivism include the long-running attack by the group Anonymous on the Church of Scientology starting in 2008,[9] attacks on Australian government websites by individuals upset by government plans to censor the Internet,[10] and the continuing saga of the Wikileaks exposure of hundreds of thousands of classified documents.[11] Cause may also take the form of individuals launching a cyber attack against assets of a foreign country or even their own country in response to government actions that the individuals find objectionable. This specific instance of cyber attacks motivated by cause defines the actions of the civilian cyber warrior.

Entertainment is probably the least known and least common motivation for malicious online acts. Its origins probably emanate from the early beginnings of the hacker community. During these early days, humor often served a functional purpose in sharing common values by constructing humorous stories and tales that contained plays on technical terms and concepts. Humor also functioned as a mild form of social control — playing a humorous prank or joke on another hacker or system administrator often brought a bit of humility to the victim and returned a sense of balance to the social situation. Compromising a machine and leaving a humorous taunt directed at its system administrator for the lack of security controls at the compromised machine was a not-too-uncommon event.

Entertainment as a motivation for acts — malicious or not — appeared to decline for some time after the early years but has recently made a resurgence. This increase in incidences of the entertainment motivation may be due in part to the preponderance of potential victims — the influx of less technical individuals into the hacking community as well as the tidal wave of technically challenged people pouring onto the web has likely facilitated the popular return of this motivation.

The final motivation is that of status. The hacking community can be described as a strong meritocracy.[12] The position of individuals in the status hierarchy of their hacking group depends upon the level of technical skills and expertise they possess relative to other members of the group. The higher the level of expertise, the higher the status of the individual is in that hacking group. Note that this positive relationship is also salient when an individual in one hacking group is compared to another hacker in the larger hacking community. The person with the higher level of skills possesses the relatively higher status.

As was the case with the entrance to social group motivation, the validation of one's expertise and thus one's status within the hierarchy can be difficult to achieve. The difficulties in proving authorship of an elegant piece of code, especially to someone outside one's normal hacking group, make this avenue of validation more problematic. One avenue that does appear to work is the acquisition of status through contests of skill, which often occurs at hacker conventions. Typically these are some variation of "capture the flag" contests, in which the objective of the contest is to use your hacking skills and expertise to compromise computer systems in order to typically search out and find a catch phrase or encryption key—the possession of which provides evidence that the contestant possesses the requisite knowledge and skill to compromise the computer and acquire the flag.

A similar exercise involving employment of malicious online acts in the wild can also lead to status acquisition and validation. One example of this is the acquisition of secret documents as a means to gain status. In this situation, one assumes that the secret documents have such value that they are heavily protected by a number of sophisticated means often in some sort of defense in-depth configuration. In order to come into possession of electronic copies of these secret documents, the malicious actor must use a significant amount of technical expertise and skill to break into the server without detection and exfiltrate copies of the secret documents.

One interesting consequence of obtaining status this way is that in the end, status exists within the possession of the secret documents. That is, these documents are status objects—they are items that in and of themselves impart status and have status. If the malicious actor publicizes or distributes the secret documents to his or her friends, then that actor in effect expends the status value that these documents have. Once they become collectively owned, they lose their status value and, consequently, the malicious actor loses status at the same time. This is one reason why, perhaps, in the case of Wikileaks, the principal actor in the incident—Julian Assange—was loathe to disclose all of the documents at once because he would have expended all of their status value and would have subsequently lost most of the status that was associated with their exclusive possession.

THE EMERGENCE OF THE CIVILIAN CYBER WARRIOR

The past few years have been witness to a significant focus on cyber-based threats. The realization of the vulnerability of the nation's critical infrastructures and the military to digitally based attacks has generated a flurry of interest and activity both by parties with substantial interests in the area—such as governmental entities carrying out national security directives—and within the military, where they deploy not only defensive strategies, but offensive strategies as well. The cyber arena has turned into the next battlefield.

The focus on the malicious actors targeting critical infrastructures in most of these scenarios has been directed at the elements of foreign nation-state intelligence organizations or military forces and previously identified foreign terrorist groups.[13] What has often been lost in the rush to protect critical infrastructures from digital attack is the idea that isolated individuals or small groups of individuals are, to a great extent, an unseen emerging threat vector to the nation's critical infrastructure.

What are the possible social dynamics behind this emerging threat? One central theme may be how technology is driving shifts in power relationships between nation-states and individuals. Foucault discusses at length the relationship between knowledge and power.[14] His argument might extend to the power-knowledge relationship within the possession of expert knowledge of technical aspects of integral digital control and communications systems embedded within national critical infrastructure. As Mathews observes, "information technologies disrupt hierarchies, spreading power among more people and groups."[15]

The key concept here is that perhaps for the first time in history, a regular civilian can effectively attack a nation-state—in this case through a cyber attack on some component of that nation-state's critical infrastructure. "Effective" in this sense means that the attack can cause significant widespread damage and has a reasonably high probability of success and a low probability of the perpetrator being apprehended. While some might argue that political assassination might already be an existing instance of this, the questions surrounding the probability of success and certainly around avoiding being apprehended make this less likely to be the case.

An example of how this shift in the balance of power between nation-state and individual may help the reader grasp the magnitude of the social-psychological shifts in thinking. Imagine that you are a citizen of country A and the government of country B is the direct causal agent for some significant actions that negatively affect your homeland and its people. Prior to the emergence of the Internet, an individual might write a letter to the President of country B and tell him or her why they object to Country B's actions. What is the likely result? Probably nothing happens that changes the actions or consequences of country B.

So this individual joins individuals who have similar feelings and meet at the embassy of country B to protest. What is the likely outcome of this action? The individual is likely to be arrested or injured by the crowd or police action without it having any real effect on country B. As the next step in the escalation, this individual cashes out his or her bank account and travels to country B, obtains some explosives and plots to damage a government building. Again, the outcome is likely not to be favorable. There is a reasonable chance that the individual will be detected by intelligence agents and/or law enforcement and arrested before he or she has the opportunity to carry out the plan. Another possible outcome is that the individual ends up blowing him or herself up while preparing the explosive device. Finally, even if the individual manages to execute the plot, he or she is likely to be arrested and, while the damage to the target might be significant, in an overall sense the nation-state and people of Country B are intact.

This example just reinforces the idea that a cyber attack on a national asset is a much more attractive path, because it likely has significantly more favorable outcomes to the malicious actor. If this is the case, then why haven't widespread incidents involving isolated individuals launching serious cyber attacks against national critical infrastructures occurred more often? Rogers suggests that it is because criminals have been "reluctant to cross certain ethical boundaries" that perhaps terrorists are willing to cross.[16] A more likely reason is that this potential shift in the power relationship between individuals and the nation-state has just not reached cultural salience. As the salience of the shift in power balance diffuses into the more general population, in combination with the development and distribution adaptation of sophisticated cyber attack tools for less technical end users, the pool of potential malicious attackers who pose threats to online systems and critical infrastructures steadily grows.

Eventually one may begin to see the consequences of this sequence of events; hence, the importance of understanding more about the potential emerging threat from the civilian cyber warrior. One of the first things that one might want to investigate in the chain of actions for a terrorist act is the initial starting point where individuals begin thinking about and rehearsing in their minds the nature, method, and target for the terrorist attack. What does one know about the propensity of individuals in the more general population to contemplate a terrorist act? What would be the magnitude or severity of damage that someone might consider justified? There is a paucity of research focusing on this area, especially from a cyber attack perspective. The following analyses are some preliminary results from a recent, ongoing study of severity predictors of an attack on a foreign country's critical infrastructure, and the severity levels of an attack directed at one's own homeland.

METHODOLOGY

The following analyses use preliminary data collected from a study by Holt and Kilger.[17] The sample for this study comes from undergraduate and graduate students at a large Midwestern U.S. university. Students received an email inviting them to participate in the study; embedded within the email was a link to the online survey. A preliminary sample of 357 students completed the survey for the purposes of this analysis. The survey itself consisted of: measures for the level of technical expertise; hours spent online; questions about previous history of ethical conduct using computers; nationalism; country considered to be one's homeland; out-group antagonism measures; demographics; and other relevant measures.

The study design was a 2 x 2 factorial design. The first factor is type of attack—cyber or physical. One of the objectives of the study was to investigate the potential relationship between cyber and physical attacks on critical infrastructure. The second factor was the target country. The target country could be a nation-state that the respondent did not consider to be his or her country or homeland—that is, a foreign target. Alternatively, the target country could be a nation-state that the respondent stated was his or her homeland or own country—that is, a homeland target. The homeland target was felt to be especially relevant in gaining some understanding of which independent variables might be associated with an attack on one's own domestic critical infrastructure. The study design appears in Table 3-1.

	Target of Attack	
Type of Attack	**Foreign Country**	**Homeland**
Cyber	Cell 1	Cell 2
Physical	Cell 4	Cell 3

Table 3-1. Dependent Variable Design.

The dependent variable was the severity of the attack that the respondent felt was appropriate for the individual scenario outlined in each of the four study cells. The scenario for a physical attack on a foreign country had the following instructions to the respondent:

> Imagine that the country of Bagaria has recently promoted national policies and taken physical actions that have had negative consequences to the country that you most closely associate as your home country or homeland. These policies and actions have also resulted in significant hardships for the people in your home country. What actions do you think would be appropriate for you to take against Bagaria given their policies and physical actions against your home country? You may choose as many actions as you think the situation warrants. In this scenario, you may assume that you have the necessary skills to carry out any of the actions below.

Following the instructions was a set of possible actions the respondent could take. These actions were ordered from lowest severity — doing nothing — to the highest severity response — in this case, travel to Bagaria and damage a government building with an explosive device. There were eight categories in all. Note that respondents were instructed to assume that they had the abilities to carry out any of the responses. This was to ensure that they did not reject any category response because they felt they did not have the skills or logistics to carry out that action successfully. Also note that respondents were allowed to select more than one action. This conformed potential reactions to real-world situations in which multiple attacks might be contemplated as well as to provide for more layers of complexity within the dependent variable.

The cyber attack scenario had similar instructions but, of course, had a different set of category responses available for the respondent to select. Here are the instructions for the second part of the foreign target country scenario:

> Aside from physical activity, what online activities do you think would be appropriate for you to take against Bagaria given their policies and physical actions against your home country? You may choose as many actions as you think the situation warrants. In this scenario, you may assume that you have the necessary skills to carry out any of the actions below.

There were nine possible response categories ordered by level of severity, ranging from doing nothing to compromising a nuclear power plant with the subsequent release of a small amount of radiation. Again, respondents could assume they had the skills necessary to carry out the attack. They also could—as was the case for physical attack responses—select multiple attacks with differing levels of severity.

The remaining two cells of the design involved retaliation against the respondent's home country infrastructure (e.g., domestic terrorist attack) for actions that his or her homeland or home country had taken against its own people. Here are the scenario instructions for the physical homeland attack:

> Imagine that the country that you most closely associate as your home country or homeland has recently promoted national policies and taken physical actions that have had negative consequences to your home country. These policies and actions have resulted in significant hardships for the people in your home country. What actions do you think would be appropriate for you to take against your home country given their policies and physical actions? You may choose as many actions as you think the situation warrants. In this scenario, you may assume that you have the necessary skills to carry out any of the actions below.

These instructions were followed by the same set of eight potential responses as found in the physical attack measure and ordered once again by severity from low to high. Similarly, the cyber attack scenario on the respondent's own homeland or home country had the following instructions:

> Aside from physical activity, what online activities do you think would be appropriate for you to take against your home country given their policies and physical actions? You may choose as many actions as you think the situation warrants. In this scenario, you may assume that you have the necessary skills to carry out any of the actions below.

Again, these scenario instructions had the same set of cyber attack responses as was the case for the cyber attack against Bagaria's critical infrastructure.

Because all of the respondents provided answers to each of the four scenarios, this study design facilitated the examination of a number of important variations in the nature of the attack of an individual on a nation-state as well as the potential relationship between the severity of potential cyber attacks and physical attacks.

RESULTS AND DISCUSSION

The results presented in this chapter are preliminary, because of the fact that more data are being collected for the study. In addition, the authors of the study are still engaged in developing and testing a number of multivariate statistical models incorporating a number of independent predictor variables available in the data. However, because of the unique nature of this study, some initial descriptive results and simple univariate tests will be reported here.

First, an examination of the frequency distribution for the dependent variables for each of the four cells in the study is useful. The response frequencies for a physical attack on a foreign country appear in Table 3-2.

Action	Percent Response
Do nothing—let your country work it out on its own	37.8%
Write a letter to government of Bagaria protesting their actions	53.6%
Participate in a protest at an anti-Bagaria rally	56.6%
Travel to Bagaria and protest at their country's capitol building	23.8%
Travel to Bagaria and confront a Bagarian senior government official about their policies	20.0%
Travel to Bagaria and sneak into a military base to write slogans on buildings and vehicles	1.3%
Travel to Bagaria and physically damage an electrical power substation	2.6%
Travel to Bagaria and damage a government building with an explosive device	0.9%

Table 3-2. Physical Attack Frequencies on Foreign Country.

Fewer than 38 percent of respondents felt that doing nothing was an appropriate response to the scenario. The most popular responses appeared to be writing a letter (53.6 percent) or protesting at a rally against Bagaria (56.6 percent). Interestingly, a nontrivial percentage of respondents would consider traveling to Bagaria to participate in some sort of civil disobedience—either protesting in the capitol (23.8 percent) or confronting a senior government official (20.0 percent). Finally, a small but nonetheless troubling number of respondents would consider sneaking onto a military base (1.3 percent), damaging a power station (2.6 percent), or damaging a Bagarian government building with an explosive device (0.9 percent[18]). Now compare this to the responses that an individual respondent would make in conducting a cyber attack against a nation-state. Table 3-3 below reveals the frequency distribution for a cyber attack on a foreign country.

About 36 percent of the respondents indicated that doing nothing in terms of mounting a cyber attack against Bagaria was an acceptable response. Interestingly, over 75 percent of the respondents felt that posting a comment criticizing the Bagarian government was an appropriate response. This should not be surprising, given the involvement of a large proportion of the online population in social networks. It may also suggest that social networks may serve a functional purpose in providing a nondestructive way in which individuals can register their displeasure at a government or nation-state.

Action	Percent Response
Do nothing —let your country work it out on its own	36.2%
Post a comment on a social networking website like Facebook or Twitter that criticizes the Bagarian government	75.3%
Deface the personal website of an important Bagarian government official	11.2%
Deface an important official Bagarian government website	10.2%
Compromise the server of a Bagarian bank and withdraw money to give to the victims of their policies and actions	5.1%
Search Bagarian government servers for secret papers that you might be able to use to embarrass the Bagarian government	8.5%
Compromise one or more Bagarian military servers and make changes that might temporarily affect their military readiness	6.4%
Compromise one of Bagaria's regional power grids, which results in a temporary power blackout in parts of Bagaria	2.6%
Compromise a nuclear power plant system, which results in a small release of radioactivity in Bagaria	0.4%

Table 3-3. Cyber Attack Frequencies on Foreign Country.

Moving up the severity scale in Table 3-3, a nontrivial number of respondents would engage in some sort of website defacement — 11.2 percent would deface the website of a specific government official, while 10.2 percent would deface a more general Bagarian government website. While website defacement generally is considered rather modest damage as far as cyber attacks go, it is still an illegal act and can cause significant embarrassment to the targeted government.

The remaining response categories in Table 3-3 are cyber attacks that are more serious in nature. A little over 5 percent of the respondents would attack a Bagarian financial institution and distribute the stolen funds to victims of the Bagarian government's actions.

In addition, about 8.5 percent of respondents would steal secret government documents to embarrass the Bagarian government à la the Wikileaks incident.

Now looking at attacks that were more directly focused upon a nation-state itself, about 6.4 percent of respondents would consider a cyber attack against a foreign country's military as an appropriate response to actions taken by that country. Finally, looking at cyber attacks that were more specifically focused on a country's critical infrastructure, 2.6 percent of respondents would consider an attack on another country's electrical grid as an appropriate response, while 0.4 percent of respondents would consider attacking a nuclear power plant in a foreign country as appropriate retaliation for acts committed by that foreign country.

An initial examination of the severity of physical attacks and cyber attacks that respondents feel were appropriate to launch against a foreign country brings both good news and bad news to the table. On the one hand, the vast majority of respondents select only responses that had minor or no consequences to the targeted foreign country. On the other hand, there are a nontrivial number of respondents who personally advocated the use of physical and cyber attacks against a foreign country that would have some moderate to very serious consequences. While there is some comfort to be had in the fact that expressing intentions to commit terrorist acts is only the first link in the behavioral chain from ideation to the execution of an attack, and bearing in mind that this is a scenario-based situation, even a small incidence of individuals who would consider some of the most serious acts is troubling. This suggests that the emergence of the civilian cyber warrior (and perhaps the physical attack counterpart) is an event that should be taken into account when developing policies and distributing resources across national priorities to protect national critical infrastructure.

In contrast to the previous scenarios, in which feelings of nationalism may have played a substantial part in the motivation of individuals to react with more severe physical or cyber attack responses against a foreign nation-state, attacks against one's own country go against many of these nationalistic sensibilities. Nonetheless, domestic terrorism has in recent years gained significant national attention, both in the press as well as within federal law enforcement agencies.

The particular design of this study introduces an additional interesting but valuable complexity to this and future analyses. Approximately 10.4 percent of the respondents completing the survey identified themselves as having a homeland that was not the United States. Therefore, the homeland that they referred to in these next two scenarios was not the United States but rather a foreign country. This means that it is possible to make comparisons of attacks on the homeland when that homeland is the United States and when it is a foreign country. This may provide some additional perspective on cross-cultural differences in the civilian cyber warrior phenomenon.[19]

The first scenario is the one featuring a physical attack against one's own homeland. Table 3-4 displays the frequency distribution for the same response set that was used in the physical attack against a foreign country scenario discussed earlier.

Action	Percent Response
Do nothing—let your country work it out on its own	28.9%
Write a letter to government of Bagaria protesting their actions	68.9%
Participate in a protest at an anti-Bagaria rally	60.0%
Travel to Bagaria and protest at their country's capitol building	51.5%
Travel to Bagaria and confront a Bagarian senior government official about their policies	28.5%
Travel to Bagaria and sneak into a military base to write slogans on buildings and vehicles	2.1%
Travel to Bagaria and physically damage an electrical power substation	1.7%
Travel to Bagaria and damage a government building with an explosive device	0.9%
Compromise a nuclear power plant system, which results in a small release of radioactivity in Bagaria	0.4%

**Table 3-4. Physical Attack Frequencies
on Homeland.**

Approximately 28.9 percent of respondents stated that doing nothing to their homeland was an appropriate response. Interestingly, this percentage was substantially smaller than that found in the foreign country example (37.8 percent). Perhaps one reason this is the case is because of the potency of negative feelings that an individual feels when one's own country commits acts against its own citizens.

Following that pattern, substantially more respondents selected writing a letter (68.9 percent) or attending a protest rally (60.0 percent) against their own country than was the case when the offending nation-state was a foreign country. Similarly, more people were willing to travel to their own capitol city and either protest (51.5 percent) or confront their own government official (28.5 percent) than in the foreign country physical attack scenario. Vandalizing the military property belonging to one's own armed forces had an incidence of 2.1 percent, while attacking one's own national critical infrastructure had incidence rates of 1.7 percent for an attack on the power grid and 0.9 percent for an attack on a nuclear plant. A comparison of these last three attack responses between the foreign country as target and the homeland as target did not appear to reveal a consistent pattern, as was the case for other scenarios.

The final scenario involved cyber attacks against one's own country or homeland. The frequency distribution for this scenario appears in Table 3-5.

Almost 36 percent of respondents felt that doing nothing was an appropriate response when considering a cyber attack on their homeland. Again, about 75 percent of respondents would post a critical comment about their own country on a social network — very similar to the foreign country cyber attack scenario. Defacing the website of a specific government official in their own government received a 12.8 percent response, while defacing a more general government website was chosen by 11.5 percent of respondents as an appropriate response. Approximately 4.3 percent of respondents would extract funds from a bank based in their own country to distribute to the victims of aggressive action on the part of their own homeland.

Action	Percent Response
Do nothing—let your country work it out on its own	35.7%
Post a comment on a social networking website like Facebook or Twitter that criticizes your home country's government	75.3%
Deface the personal website of an important government official for your home country	12.8%
Deface an important official government website for your home country	11.5%
Compromise the server of a bank and withdraw money to give to the victims of the government's policies and actions	4.3%
Search your home country's government servers for secret papers that you might be able to use to embarrass the government	8.9%
Compromise one or more of your home country's military servers and make changes that might temporarily affect their military readiness	4.7%
Compromise one of your home country's regional power grids, which results in a temporary power blackout in parts of your home country	1.7%
Compromise a nuclear power plant system, which results in a small release of radioactivity in your home country	0.9%

Table 3-5. Cyber Attack Frequencies on Homeland.

A surprising 8.9 percent would consider actions akin to a Wikileaks event, in which they would attempt to exfiltrate copies of secret documents in order to embarrass their own government. Almost 5 percent would use a cyber attack to reduce the readiness of their own military forces. A little over 1.7 percent of respondents would attack their own national power grid, while just 0.9 percent suggested that attacking a nuclear power plant in their own country would be an appropriate response.

When one compares the homeland cyber attack distribution to the foreign country cyber attack scenario distribution, it seems that they are more similar in shape than the two physical attack scenario distributions. It is unclear why this might be the case; perhaps it is due to the fact that the physical attacks require actual travel for some of the foreign country responses, and that may involve more risk than the cyber attacks in which it does not matter where the attacking individual is geographically located.

Now that we have an idea of the frequency distribution of the variables of interest, some simple, initial univariate analyses may prove useful here. One of the obvious questions concerns the hypothesis that there might be some difference between the severity levels of an attack based on whether the target was a foreign country or someone's own homeland. Controlling for the type of attack facilitates the analysis, because the response scales involved in the comparison are identical. For these and subsequent analyses, given the multiple response nature of the response variables, one should utilize the maximum severity response as the indicator of the severity of the response chosen by the respondent. That is, the study will use the most severe response of all the responses the respondent selects for a particular scenario. A simple parametric dependent sample paired t-test can be employed for these comparisons. Severity scores range from one to eight for physical attack responses and from one to nine for cyber attacks, with the highest value being the most severe response.

If you compare target countries—foreign country versus homeland—the first thing to notice in table 3-6 is that all the means have reasonably small values in comparison with the range of the scale. This is the result of most of the respondents selecting attack responses that were modest in their level of severity.

If there is some silver lining in this cloud, it is the fact that most of the respondents selected either no action or actions that had modest consequences. One would not want to live in a world where the results revealed variables near the top of the scale; however, in some less robust countries, this generalization might be false.

Comparison	Mean Severity	T	Df	Sig (2-tail)
Cyber Foreign	1.62	.57	356	.569
Cyber Homeland	1.60			
Physical Foreign	2.94	-7.80	356	<.001
Physical Homeland	3.46			

Table 3-6. Foreign Versus Homeland Target.

Interestingly, there is no evidence supporting a difference in mean attack severity between foreign and homeland targets for the cyber attack scenarios. If nationalistic factors were involved here, one would expect a more severe attack directed toward the foreign country. Perhaps the fact that one can launch this kind of attack without ever being physically close to the target may have some effect, which attenuated an individual's propensity to launch a more severe attack on one type of target than the other.

Examining the mean differences for the physical attack scenario, a statistically significant difference is detected—it appears that respondents selected a more severe level of attack for their own homeland than they would for a foreign country. Certainly, it is not traditional nationalistic factors at work here. One possible reason for this might be the strong reaction from individuals to a government whose actions hurt their own people. One might think of this as a type of nationalism turned "inside out." One of the basic functions of government is to obtain and maintain the security and safety of its people. Governments violate a very strong cultural norm when they intentionally hurt the very individuals they should protect.

Finally, given that skill plays an important role in the strong meritocracy of the hacking community, this suggests that there might be a positive relationship between the severity of an attack on a nation-state's infrastructure and the skills of the individual selecting the type of attack. A principle components factor analysis was performed on eight measures of computer skills, such as installing an operating system or handling security issues, to produce a factor score-based variable that represents claimed technical skills by the respondent.

A quick look at Table 3.7 reveals that there are weak but statistically significant positive correlations between the skill factor variable and attack severity across all four attack scenarios. This suggests, as one might expect, a positive correlation between cyber attack severity and skill level for an individual. What is more surprising is that these correlations also exist between technical skills and physical attack severity. In addition, these weak but detectable correlations persist across both homeland and foreign country targets. Although caution must be taken because these are preliminary data, this finding may suggest that individuals with technical skills may pose multidimensional threats to critical infrastructure elements. It also suggests that there could be some crossover in the mode of attack for individuals. This may be especially enlightening in the scenario in which individuals whose traditional mode of attack is cyber-based might transition to either a blend of cyber and physical attack or eventually migrate to a strictly physical attack.

Scenario	Pearsons r	Sig (1-tail)
Physical Foreign	0.096*	0.030
Physical Homeland	0.118*	0.013
Cyber Foreign	0.100*	0.030
Cyber Homeland	0.109*	0.020

Table 3-7. Correlations between Skill Factor and Attack Severity.

CONCLUSION

Hopefully, this discussion has addressed several objectives. First, it has given the reader a basic fundamental understanding of motivations associated with actors who perpetrate malicious online behaviors — knowing your enemy can be a key element in gaining a comprehensive perspective on attacks against online targets. A second objective of the study is to identify specific instances of the civilian cyber warrior as a potentially more serious threat to critical infrastructure. Finally, some simple and initial analyses on preliminary data from a recent study have provided some empirical data that can be useful in guiding further investigation.[20]

Future analyses involving multivariate analyses of the civilian cyber warrior used in this chapter are already underway, and very preliminary results suggest that some of the independent predictor variables have statistically significant relationships to attack severity. Hopefully, this research will encourage others to pursue similar areas of investigation with the objective of better predicting the level of threat that the nation's critical infrastructure faces.

ENDNOTES - CHAPTER 3

1. Raoul Chiesa, Stefania Ducci, and Silvio Ciappi, *Profiling Hackers: The Science of Criminal Profiling as Applied to the World of Hacking*, Boca Raton, FL: Auerbach Publishing, 2009.

2. Marc Rogers, *The Development of a Meaningful Hacker Taxonomy: A Two Dimensional Approach*, West Lafayette, IN: Center for Education and Research in Information Assurance and Security, Purdue University, 2005.

3. Tom Parker, Eric Shaw, Ed Stroz, Mathew Devost, and Marcus Sachs, *Cyber Adversary Characterization: Auditing the Hacker Mind*, Rockland, MA: Syngress, 2004.

4. Max Kilger, Ofir Arkman, and Jeff Stutzman, "Profiling," Honeynet Project, ed., *Know Your Enemy*, 2nd Ed., Boston, MA: Addison Wesley, 2004, pp. 505-556.

5. This was based upon the counterintelligence acronym MICE, which stood for the reasons someone would betray his or her country—Money, Ideology, Compromise, and Ego.

6. Kilger, Stutzman, and Arkin, "Profiling."

7. Max Kilger, "Social Dynamics and the Future of Technology-driven Crime," in Thomas Holt and Bernadette Schell, eds., *Corporate Hacking and Technology Driven Crime: Social Dynamics and Implications,* Hershey, PA: IGI-Global, pp. 205-227.

8. *Ibid.*

9. Ryan Singel, "War Breaks Out Between Hackers and Scientology—There Can Be Only One," *Wired Threat Level*, January 23, 2008, available from *www.wired.com/threatlevel/2008/01/anonymous-attac/*.

10. Michelle Starr, "Anonymous Attacks Australian Government Over Censorship," ChannelNews Australia, October 2, 2010, available from *www.channelnews.com.au/Content_And_Management/Industry/E4C6V5V6*.

11. Xeni Jardin, "Wikileaks Releases Classified Afghanistan War Logs: 'Largest Intelligence Leak in History'," *boingboing.net*, July 25, 2010, available from *boingboing.net/2010/07/25/wikileaks-releases-c.html*.

12. Kilger, "Social Dynamics and the Future of Technology-driven Crime."

13. Dorothy Denning, "A View of Cyberterrorism Five Years Later," Kenneth Himma, ed., *Internet Security: Hacking, Counterhacking and Society,* Sudbury, MA: Jones and Bartlettt, 2007, pp. 123-140.

14. Michael Foucault, *Power/Knowledge: Selected Interviews and Other Writings 1972-1977*, Brighton, UK: Harvester Press, 1980.

15. Jessica Mathews, "Power Shift," *Foreign Affairs*, 1997, Vol. 76, No. 1, pp. 50-66.

16. Marc Rogers, "The Psychology of Cyber Terrorism," Andrew Silke, ed., *Terrorist, Victims and Society: Psychological Perspectives on Terrorism and Its Consequences*, Chichester, UK: John Wiley & Sons, Inc., 12003, pp. 77-92.

17. Thomas Holt and Max Kilger, "Understanding the Behaviors of Cyberattackers Online and Offline," Presentation at the 10th Annual Honeynet Project Workshop, Paris, France, 2011.

18. Note that respondents are able to select more than one attack response, so the percentages will sum to more than 100 percent. One must be careful to observe that another result is that the percentages in the table are not strictly additive across response categories.

19. The authors of the study are currently engaged in negotiations with researchers in several other countries to deploy the study cross-nationally.

20. Holt and Kilger.

PART II:

LAW AND CYBERCRIME

CHAPTER 4

CHANGING THE GAME:
SOCIAL AND JUSTICE MODELS
FOR ENHANCED CYBER SECURITY

Michael M. Losavio
J. Eagle Shutt
Deborah Wilson Keeling

Thanks to the City College of New York, Grove School of Engineering, the Strategic Studies Institute of the U.S. Army War College and the 2009 Cyber Infrastructure Protection Conference, and Oak Ridge National Laboratory and its Cyberspace Sciences and Information Intelligence Research (CSIIR) Group and CSIIR Workshop 2010 for helping develop these themes.

INTRODUCTION

To change the game in cyber security, we should consider criminal justice and social education models to secure the highly distributed elements of the information network, extend the effective administration of justice to cybercrime, and embed security awareness and competence in engineering and common computer practice. This chapter examines models of such behavior.

A broad approach is needed, since no single group of agencies can combat cybercrime alone.[1] The approach to cyber security and cybercrime must change and expand. Traditional models for combating internal and transnational threats can assist with cyber security, even as information networks have expanded the risks to information security.

Physical security itself is insufficient, when an inmate in a correctional facility can crack the network from within the jail.[2] Information control via ever-smaller handheld devices is increasingly difficult. For example, almost 53 percent of inmates in one state's correctional facilities misused electronics.[3] See Figure 4-1.

Although the nation's homes may be castles, protected as no other space in American civil society is, that may not be true in regard to cyber security. As the 2003 *National Strategy to Secure Cyberspace* observed, these houses may offer targets of choice as sources of gain and tools for attack.[4] The Internet puts the criminals and terrorists worldwide at our electronic doorstep, magnifying the risks and problems in addressing these information security problems. Cyber security must address how to achieve security in such a disparate, target-rich environment as that of worldwide computing.

The *National Cyber Leap Year Co-Chairs Report* addressed the need for "game changing" approaches.[5] One novel approach used "Cyber Economics" for developing a market-type engagement in cyber security issues. This approach proposed four economic strategies for examination via research and policy implementation for "game-changing" solutions in cyber security:

1. Mitigating Incomplete Information: Mitigate incomplete and asymmetric information barriers that hamper efficient security decisionmaking at the individual and organizational levels.

2. Incentives and Liabilities: Leverage incentives and impose or redistribute liabilities to promote secure behavior and decisionmaking among stakeholders.

3. Reduction of Attackers' Profitability: Promote legal, technical, and social changes that reduce attackers' revenues or increase their costs, thus lowering the overall profitability (and attractiveness) of cybercrime.

4. Market Enforceability: Ensure that proposed changes are enforceable with market mechanisms.[6]

Incentives and new liabilities would include expanded vendor, Internet service provider (ISP), registrar and registry **accountability**, **liability,** and **rewards** for protective conduct, or the lack thereof (emphasis added). The report further notes that cyber security metrics are "poorly investigated," in that there is no accepted foundation for: (1) the information to collect; (2) the use of such information; and, (3) the weight of such information as to elements of uncertainty, inaccuracy, and error in its collection.[7]

Similarly, there are challenges to the orthodoxy of security engineering education that contend certain "myths" about security, such as the sufficiency of purely technical solutions and defense-in-depth strategies. These myths impede the creation of effective cyber security systems.[8]

CRIMINAL JUSTICE MODELS

The Application of Criminal Justice Models to Cyber Security.

In 2000, the Strategic Studies Institute (SSI) of the U.S. Army War College (USAWC) published a discussion on how criminal justice models might integrate into cyber security systems.[9] The techniques and resources of state and local law enforcement and criminal justice entities could fit within national response. This seems appropriate, as communication networks have blurred national boundaries. The discussion also addresses the risks such an enmeshed world would create to civil society and its liberties, in which responses to attack risk "profound constitutional and security challenges" for the United States.[10]

Safety and security require more than technical protections and police response. They need a critical blend of those elements with individual practice and social norms. Social norms matched with formal institutions enhance public safety; this also holds true in the cyber realm.

Informal and formal modes of controlling and limiting deviant behavior are essential for effective security.[11] Laws, procedures, and criminal justice agencies are all modes of formal social control. Attitudes, values, and actions of individuals represent potentially powerful informal modes. A community with a high degree of both modes will have a strong overall level of social control. These efforts must be incentivized and empowered at all levels. Where there is consonance in these two modes, there will be the greatest security.

Examples: Routine Activity Theory/Opportunity Theory and Displacement Theory.

This study suggests that the routine activity theory/opportunity theory and displacement theory — frameworks for analyzing crime in communities — are ways to conceptualize and pattern the benefits of informal social control on cyber security.[12]

Routine activities theory (RAT) posits that each of three elements contributes to a heightened or lessened risk: a suitable target, a lack of guardianship, and a motivated offender.[13] The absence of one of these elements reduces the risk of misconduct, whereas their convergence increases it. For cyber security, the analysis should equally consider the availability of suitable targets, a presence or lack of suitable guardians, and an increase or decrease in the number of motivated offenders, particularly those seeking financial gain or state advantages.

Changes in attitudes among those who use these cyber systems can increase suitable guardians and reduce suitable targets, thereby changing the risk equation. This is a vital part of informal social control that must develop with and without technical supplements. There is no technical "patch" for ignorance.[14]

The overall power of social control is a function of both formal and informal controls.[15] Laws, public policies, and law enforcement exemplify elements of formal social control, whereas community attitudes and norms exemplify informal control. While both spheres can impede crime, states with the greatest levels of control will have high degrees of both formal and informal social control.

In cyber security contexts, high levels of informal social control are essential to deter cyber attacks, particularly since attackers exploit the anonymity and distance-collapsing features of cyberspace as vectors for attack. For example, open source software practices have led to questions regarding cyber security. Yet, this software represents a collaborative social network that self-organizes and grows as a preferentially attached network.[16] Such preferential attachment to cyber security can promote a distributed security regime through commitments to competent and suitable guardianship of the nodes and network around the subject code project.

Online social networks suggest opportunities for the examination of RAT-based security promotion. Facebook, MySpace, and LiveJournal are all online social networks that promote cyber security both within and outside their domains. The observation, reporting, and notice/alert possibilities of network members who are competent and committed to security and protection can expand the guardianship network for anomalous behavior; they may also serve to reduce target vulnerability directly.

The information social network for the open source encyclopedia, *Wikipedia*, is another example of a community of guardians that has been successful in securing the information it presents. It may also serve as an example of risks due to its uncertainty of information assurance in topic areas lacking extensive guardian participation. The possibilities of such social networks for enhancing cyber security are significant, if realized. Alan Mislove, Massimiliano Marcon, Krishna Gummadi, Peter Druschel, and Bobby Bhattacharjee found that online social networks have small-world and scale-free properties based on power-law; these would indicate potential for the expansion of a guardian security regime.[17] Others contend that though some aspects of RAT can apply to criminal activity involving computing systems, there are key differences that limit the utility of the model.[18] The collapse of the social network may degrade the security of information.[19] There must be vigilance in seemingly normal activity used to mask an attack.[20]

Consider M. Felson and R. V. Clarke's 10 principles of crime opportunity theory:[21]

1. Opportunities play a role in causing all crime.
2. Crime opportunities are highly specific.
3. Crime opportunities are concentrated in time and space.
4. Crime opportunities depend on everyday movements of activity.
5. One crime produces opportunities for another.
6. Some products offer more tempting crime opportunities.
7. Social and technological changes produce new crime opportunities.
8. Crime can be prevented by reducing opportunities.
9. Reducing opportunities does not usually displace crime.
10. Focused opportunity reduction can produce wider declines in crime.

Figure 4-2. Ten Principles of Opportunity and Crime.

These principles may be mapped to a variety of technical and nontechnical factors that enhance or diminish cyber security. Identifying opportunities and

mitigating them are a major focus of information security research in finding technical vulnerabilities of
systems. These vulnerabilities are specific and limited
to the user space of a specific system, particularly
those of typical system use. Once an exploit is found
and used, its use will be replicated in other situations.
Mitigation of these exploits may be both technical and
nontechnical.

Certainly the expansion of social conduct into the
online world has produced new crime opportunities
within technology. As in other situations of expanding crime and social deviancy, the application to reduce these opportunities can have a beneficial effect
in reducing cybercrime. Technical solutions certainly
help, just as strong doors and locks help, but other factors, such as personal vigilance for self and neighbors
and assured punitive response, can help as much or
even more. These measures accord with the solution
features suggested in the *National Cyber Leap Year
Co-chairs Report*.[22]

Another application of criminological principles
to cyber security relates to the use of criminal profiling and behavioral analysis.[23] The reactive use of
these techniques, much like the use of technical digital forensics in network settings, serves to focus an
investigation and response in particular areas and on
particular individuals. This, in some cases, may be as
limited as the method of operation (*modus operandi*, or
"MO") of a particular miscreant. But the reactive use
goes beyond this to distinctive behaviors of individuals that are *a priori* and may lead to the use of particular operational methods or tools.

Proactive use of profiling deters, or prevents,
crimes such as drug courier profiling. Frank Greitzer,
Deborah Frincke, and Mariah Zabrieski discuss this in

relation to the application of traditional security techniques to the identification of insider cyber security threats.[24] The set of circumstances that have been associated with motives or disinhibitions leading to insider criminal activity, such as fraud or violence, may also match with insider cyber security breaches. The researchers note that, "Assessing ability, opportunity, and motivation is a primary decisionmaking task underlying the threat analysis."[25] These factors may then map to information and network metrics as part of an enhanced alert for potential or actual threats to information security.

J. L. Krofcheck and M. G. Gelles,[26] note these non-technical life factors and characteristics as risk indicators for insider cyber security threats:

- Non-U.S. citizen,
- Major life change,
- Access to classified information,
- System administrator rights,
- High level of computer skills and knowledge,
- Intermittent work history,
- Family/marriage issues,
- Legal issues,
- Credit/debt problems,
- Past or current arrest/criminal activity, and
- Strong interest in Blackhat community.

In turn, these indicators also present ethical and administrative issues with this security analysis, creating possible problems due to the possible invasion of privacy, and false suspicions that undermine both the reputations and morale of staff.

But there is the risk of creating hyper-romantic myths of profiling effectiveness. No profile alone has led to an arrest; rather, it is a directive tool of investigation that may be most effective when pychopathologies are present.[27]

SOCIAL AND EDUCATION MODELS

Cyber Security Awareness through Teaching Community Engagement.

Opportunities for invasion are reduced when a system user recognizes the risks and personally mitigates them. This could be as simple as not opening an email attachment from an unknown correspondent or permitting an unknown program permission to run. Such security could be achieved through the engagement of computer engineering students to broaden their understanding of their responsibilities to both the profession and to the public.

As with community safety relating to violent crime, cyber security requires effort and engagement, including general computing competence. But, there is little formal training in this area for the general public who are the most at risk. A model for such an engagement that would provide this training and awareness appears below.

The National Science Foundation-funded effort produced the *Information Assurance and Security Ethics in Complex Systems: Interdisciplinary Perspectives,* to demonstrate the value of an interdisciplinary approach to cyber security development. This approach compiles many different and highly novel perspectives on information security and assurance, and encompasses a broader review of the consequences of failure than is traditionally addressed.

This collection begins with the challenge of how people view any problem and the natural tendency toward self-reference in framing issues. This may be quickly placed in the cyber security space, with computer engineering students directed to identify threats and responses. Through use of chapters dealing with "Social/Ethical Issues in Predictive Insider Threat Monitoring," "Peer-to-Peer Networks: Interdisciplinary Challenges for Interconnected Systems," and "Responsibility for the Harm and Risk of Software Security Flaws," students may then understand the greater complexity they face in security solutions as well as the legal and ethical consequences of failure in cyber security. Through their novelty, these perspectives push students to uncomfortable discussions that, in turn, may lead to better understanding of the challenges faced in order to achieve effective cyber security. These difficult discussions need to take place if there is to be effective security for our information and people.

Extending this information beyond the classroom becomes the next challenge.

An Information Security Model.

One model for expanding the discussion into real-life application implements the use of computer engineering students to handle community projects relating to cyber security. The Department of Computer Engineering and Computer Science at the University of Louisville introduced a community engagement/community-based learning/service learning component to its 500-level course on information security in the summer of 2009. This course, in addition to examining engineering, technical, and scientific foundations of data security, addressed issues relating to the administrative and practical implementation of secure computing practices. The community engagement/service learning component required the students to examine user responsibilities and their computer related needs. The students also implement a program to teach non-expert computer users safe and secure computing practices. This, in turn, allowed them to examine the foundations essential to information security and how to teach and communicate with others. The University of Louisville Engineering School has an extensive cooperative education program requiring students to work in industry. This community engagement/service learning component, however, requires the students to examine the interaction of computing systems with typical, non-expert users.

Service learning and community engagement components in 2009-10 courses on Information Security were directed at "authentic" issues of secure broad community deployment, the use of broadband services, the security of existing personal and small business systems, and user training.[28] In addition to laboratory and design work, students created and implemented a detailed, low-level training program to community groups on user risk, conduct, and responsibilities related to online security. Training was administered in single presentations to various age groups ranging from elderly and retired individuals to elementary school students, with a focus on low-income communities. The following year, this program evolved into small group/one-on-one sessions with the targeted users.

Data Analysis and Outcomes for Students.

An assessment of student learning outcomes revealed that through the service learning/community engagement component, students had enhanced learning related to issues of information security.[29] Of the respondents, 66 percent agreed that the engagement component, ". . . helped me either connect what I learned to real-life situations or contributed to knowledge in the discipline." Three-fourths agreed that it, ". . . provided me an opportunity to apply skills and knowledge I have gained from my major courses." The 2009 community presentation on information security scored well when compared with other components in connecting learning to real-life problems, as shown in Figure 4-3.

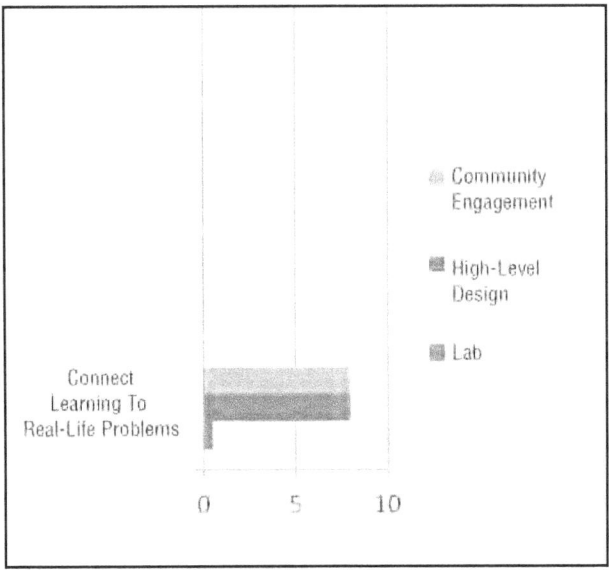

Figure 4-3. Effectiveness in Connecting Learning to Real-Life Problems.

The program allowed students to address authentic issues in the discipline of Information Security, as detailed in Figure 4-4, with nearly three times as many students finding the community engagement component connected them to an authentic experience within their discipline as compared with the system design or laboratory components.

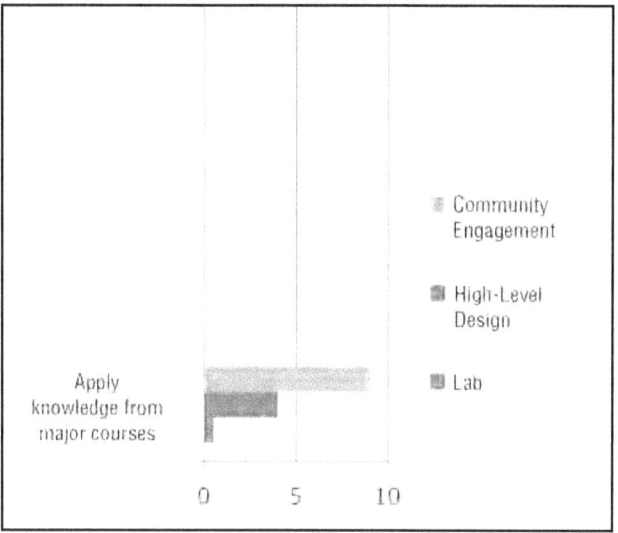

Figure 4-4. Application of Skills and Knowledge from Major Courses.

This indicates value in such teaching and learning components for the students themselves.

The benefit and improvement in cyber security by those in the community receiving the training was studied in 2010 via surveys of the several site supervisors. Those surveys similarly indicated positive experiences with the training. The respondents agreed that the presentations covered new information on security for their target groups and improved the safe practices of those using computers.

The response from the site supervisor for the senior citizens residential facility provided anecdotal comments that indicated additional concerns about both a desire to access online services and a need for fundamental skills. These comments, from individuals ranging from 67 years of age to 88 years of age, noted:

- I want to get online when I learn the basics of how to use a computer. Seniors are unable to help other seniors. They do not have the patience or skills to explain things to other seniors. Every time you turn around, you need to have a computer. You can't enter a contest or shop online. If you want to learn more about a particular news story, they tell you to go online. Many free discount coupons are only available online.
- All my family has computers, and they talk back and forth to each other. I would love to be with them.
- Keyboard would be difficult, but I would love to do family history research.
- The students made my computer faster, much faster. We did not get into a discussion about security (the main concern was about medical information).
- I never order anything on the computer. I have heard too many stories of persons losing everything by giving out credit information.
- Students helped with setting up my games. I still have pop ups and must restart the games.

These responses demonstrate both the need and desire for skills in secure, competent computing. The program offers a way to distribute security awareness

and skills that meet the requirements of criminal justice theory and provide learning objectives within the
discipline of computer engineering.

**The National Collegiate Cyber Defense
Competition.**

The National Collegiate Cyber Defense Competition brings together students from universities who
compete regionally and then nationally to protect
computer systems from cyber attacks. Lieutenant
General Harry Raduege, Jr. (USAF, Ret.), chairman
of the Deloitte Center for Cyber Innovation and co-
chairman of the Commission on Cyber Security for the
44th presidency, has noted, "These exercises are vital
training for people who will be safeguarding the nation's systems and infrastructure."[30]
To prepare for the computer attacks of the future,
the competing students must successfully defend
their computer network against hostile attacks while
maintaining operations in regional and national competition. Attacks against their systems are conducted
by penetration testers from the industry.
This is an intensive laboratory experience for the
next generation of cyber defenders. It is another example of a social/education model for developing
cyber security skills across the operational spectrum
in an environment close to the real world, with all the
complexities, ambiguities, and stresses it entails.[31]

FUTURE DIRECTIONS

Areas of study and testing in expanding cyber
security are recommended. This must move from
concept to pilot models that one can measure for ef-

fectiveness. In the limited examples described here, data on the effectiveness of the training systems are one area that requires further study to establish firmly the benefit of this model. The testing and data on pilot projects is the next step to enhancing guardianship roles and hardening targets. For example, the Cyber Clean Center project of the Japanese Computer Emergency Response Team Coordination Center is a cross-disciplinary collaboration between JP-CERT, Trend Micro, ISPs, and various security vendors—the goal of which is to create a guardian network against botnet compromise and exploitation.

Participating ISPs operate decoy honeypot machines on their networks that serve as sensors for botnet activity. They log the Internet protocol (IP) addresses of infected machines, from which the ISPs notify the infected user of the compromise and offer a "BOT disinfestation website" with easy, clear instructions and downloadable tools to clean their compromised machines.[32] The system is dynamic, with analysts monitoring sensor activity and creating "disinfestation" tools directed toward new threats.

The activity report data for April 2010 show a cumulative number of 484,583 (7,561 for April) alert emails sent to 100,696 (3, 751 for April) recipients, with a cumulative download rate of disinfestation tools of 31.8 percent.[33] The CCC data offer an opportunity to evaluate the effectiveness of methods, such as this one in enhancing security, particularly as an application of the guardian roles in enhancing cyber security.

Melissa Hathaway, a cyber security expert during the George Bush and Barack Obama administrations, has suggested the online game "The SmokeScreen Game" as a novel way to promote secure behavior.[34] The SmokeScreen Game is a British project that lets students test life online through social media and their interactions with others in the electronic world. The SmokeScreen Game addresses lies, malice, misinformation, and criminal online conduct, allowing young people to test these parameters in a simulation before being caught in a potentially damaging reality.

Lastly, the 2011 service learning and community engagement components will continue to collect additional data on the effectiveness of this model. Computer engineering students in the junior-level course on legal, ethical, and social issues in computing have begun more fundamental work with community members on competent computing—expanding the base of skills and producing additional data on basic user needs.

CONCLUSION

Cyber security is yet another facet of security in an uncertain world, an issue people have sought to address throughout human history. It requires global attention, not a belief that "police action" can solve all risks. Cyber security can be enhanced through the use of criminal justice and social education models to secure the highly distributed elements of the information network. It can extend the effective administration of justice to cybercrime and embed security awareness and competence in the use of pervasive and ubiquitous computing via novel and creative ways to engage people in their own online cyber security.

Because this is happening swiftly in an expanding world of cyber consumers that has outstripped our traditional educational system, special efforts must be made to engage citizens in protecting this new, rich environment for learning, commerce, and society. Failure to do so will only expand the pool of victims, potential and real.

ENDNOTES - CHAPTER 4

1. Doug Hanchard, "FBI Director on Cyber Threats: We Can't Do it Alone," ZDNet, March 5, 2010.

2. USDOJ Press Release, December 22, 2009, "Former Inmate Sentenced for Hacking Prison Computer," available from *www.cybercrime.gov/janoskoSent.pdf.*

3. N. Armstrong, M Losavio, D. Keeling, "Digital System, Evidence & Forensics Issues In Correctional Environments," Proceedings of the IEEE Workshop on Systematic Approaches to Digital Forensics Engineering, 2010; D. Kane, "Cell Phones Plague Prisons," *The News & Observer,* December 5, 2008.

4. Administration of President George W. Bush, *The National Strategy to Secure Cyberspace*, 2003, available from *www.dhs.gov/xlibrary/assets/National_Cyberspace_Strategy.pdf.*

5. National Cyber Leap Year Summit 2009 Co-Chairs Report, September 16, 2009.

6. *Ibid.*

7. *Ibid.*

8. Edward B. Talbot, Deborah Frincke, Matt Bishop, "Demythifying Cybersecurity," *IEEE Security and Privacy*, Vol. 8, No. 3, 2010, p. 56-59.

9. Carolyn Pumphrey, "Introduction," Carolyn Pumphrey, ed., *Transnational Threats: Blending Law Enforcement and Military Strategies*, Carlisle, PA: Strategic Studies Institute, U.S. Army War College. 2000.

10. *Ibid.*

11. Stanley Cohen, *Visions of Social Control: Crime, Punishment, and Classification*, Cambridge, UK: Polity Press, 1985.

12. Michael Losavio, John Shutt, Deborah Keeling, "The Information Polity: Social and Legal Frameworks for Critical Cyber Infrastructure Protection," *Cyber Infrastructure Protection: Policy and Strategy*, New York: City University of New York, June, 2009; Michael Losavio, John Shutt, Deborah Keeling, Abstract, "Positing Social and Justice Models for Cyber Security," poster presentation, April , 2010, *Cyber Security and Information Intelligence Research Workshop 2010*, Oak Ridge National Laboratory, Oak Ridge, TN.

13. Marcus Felson and Ronald Clarke, *Opportunity Makes the Thief: Practical Theory for Crime Prevention*, Police Research Series, Paper 98, Barry Webb, ed., Policing and Reducing Crime Unit, Research, Development and Statistics Directorate, Home Office, London, UK; Lawrence E. Cohen and Marcus Felson, "Social Change and Crime Rate Trends: A Routine Activity Approach," *American Sociological Review*, Vol. 44, 1979, pp. 588-605; Raymond Cox, Terrance Johnson, George Richards, "Routine Activity Theory and Internet Crime," Frank Schmalleger and Michael Pittaro, eds., *Crimes of the Internet*, Upper Saddle River, NJ: Pearson Education, 2009.

14. Rob Lamb, "6 Dumbest Ideas in Computer Security — Revisited (I Disagree)," September 26, 2005, available from *elamb.org/6-dumbest-ideas-in-computer-security-revisited/*, in response to the quote attributed to Kevin Mitnick that "There is no patch for stupidity."

15. Stanley Cohen, *Visions of Social Control: Crime*.

16. Greg Madey, Vincent Freeh, Renee Tynan, "The Open Source Software Development Phenomenon: An Analysis Based On Social Network Theory," Eighth Americas Conference on Information Systems, 2002.

17. Alan Mislove, Massimiliano Marcon, Krishna Gummadi, Peter Druschel, and Bobby Bhattacharjee, "Measurement and Analysis of Online Social Networks," Proceedings of the 7th ACM SIGCOMM Conference on Internet Measurement, San Diego, CA, 2007.

18. Majid Yar, "'The Novelty of "Cybercrime': An Assessment in Light of Routine Activity Theory," *European Journal of Criminology*, Vol. 2, No. 4, 2005, pp. 407-427.

19. Paul Murphy, "Do Problems with Wikipedia Presage Social Networking's End?" *ZDNet*, July 15, 2008, available from *blogs.zdnet.com/Murphy/?p=1190*.

20. Eliot Rich *et al.*, "Simulating Insider Cyber-Threat Risks," Proceedings from International Conference of System Dynamics Society, 2005, available from *www.cert.org/insider_threat/docs/insider_threatISDC2005.pdf* .

21. Felson and Clarke, *Opportunity Makes the Thief.*

22. *National Cyber Leap Year Co-chairs Report*, September 16, 2009, available from *www.cyber.st.dhs.gov/docs/National_Cyber_Leap_Year_Summit_2009_Co-Chairs_Report.pdf.*

23. David Shoemaker and Daniel Kennedy, "Criminal Profiling and Cyber Criminal Investigations," Frank Schmalleger and Michael Pittaro, eds., *Crimes of the Internet*, London, UK: Pearson Education, 2009.

24. Frank Greitzer, Deborah Frincke, and Mariah Zabrieski, "Social/Ethical Issues in Predictive Insider Threat Monitoring," Melissa Dark, ed., *Information Assurance and Security Ethics in Complex Systems: Interdisciplinary Perspectives,* Hershey, PA: IGI Global, 2011.

25. *Ibid.*

26. J. L. Krofcheck and M. G. Gelles, *Behavioral Consultation in Personnel Security: Training and Reference Manual for Personnel Security Professionals*, Fairfax, VA: Yarrow Associates, 2005.

27. Ron Holmes and Stephen Holmes, *Profiling Violent Crimes*, 4th Ed., Thousand Oaks, CA: Sage Publications, 2009.

28. Broadband Opportunities Technology Program, National Telecommunications and Information Administration (NTIA), available from *www.ntia.doc.gov/broadbandgrants/*.

29. Adapted from S. B. Gelmon, B. A. Holland, A. Driscoll, A. Spring, and S. Kerrigan, "Assessing Service-Learning and Civic Engagement: Principles and Techniques." Providence, RI: Campus Compact and Portland State's *Capstone Student Survey*, 2001.

30. "Future Cyber Workforce Strengthened Through National Collegiate Cyber Defense Competition," Deloitte Press Release, February 4, 2011, available from *https://www.deloitte.com/view/ en_US/us/press/Press-Releases/506fc428381ed210VgnVCM2000001b 56f00aRCRD.htm*.

31. The engineering students competing for the University of Louisville in 2011 were Eric McDowell, Team Captain; Joseph Stigers, Assistant Team Captain; James Gissendaner; Henry John Paul Frederick; James Corcoran; Justin Cottrell; Joshua Chase; Jimmy Murphy; and Tu Nguyen.

32. "Attention Rousing Activities," Cyber Clean Center, Ministry of Internal Affairs and Communications and Ministry of Economy, Trade and Industry (Japan), available from *https:// www.ccc.go.jp/en_activity/index.html*.

33. "Activity Report, April, FY 2010," Cyber Clean Center, Ministry of Internal Affairs and Communications and Ministry of Economy, Trade and Industry (Japan), available from *https:// www.ccc.go.jp/en_report/201004/index.html*.

34. Melissa Hathaway, Keynote Speech, CSIIRW '10 Proceedings of the Sixth Annual Workshop on Cyber Security and Information Intelligence Research. The Smokescreen Game is available from *www.smokescreengame.com/*.

CHAPTER 5

AN INSTITUTIONAL AND DEVELOPMENTAL ANALYSIS
OF THE DATA BREACH DISCLOSURE LAWS

Melissa Dark

This chapter is based on an earlier, extended version of a chapter that appears in Melissa J. Dark, ed., "Information Assurance and Security Ethics in Complex Systems: Interdisplinary Perspectives," Hershey, PA: IGI Global, available from *www.igi-global.com*, posted by permission of the publisher.

INTRODUCTION

Although advances in computing promise substantial benefits for individuals and society, trust in computing and communications is critical in order to realize such benefits. The hope for cyber trust is to create a society in which trust enables technologies to support individual and societal needs without violating confidences and exacerbating public risks. Cyber trust, in part, depends on software and hardware technologies upon which people can justifiably rely. However, the cyber trust vision requires looking beyond technical controls to consider how other forms of social control contribute to a state of cyber trust. As information technology has become more ubiquitous and pervasive, assurance and security concerns have escalated; in response, there has been noticeable growth in public policy as a form of social control to bolster cyber trust. One can see such growth just by briefly inventorying some of the regulations enacted to protect security and privacy:

- Freedom of Information Act (1966)
- ProFair Credit Reporting Act (1970)
- Bank Secrecy Act (1970)
- Privacy Act (1974)
- Family Educational Rights and Privacy Act (FERPA) (1974)
- Right to Financial Privacy Act (1978)
- Foreign Intelligence Surveillance Act (1978)
- Electronic Communications Privacy Act (ECPA) (1986)
- Telephone Consumer Protection Act (1991)
- Communications Assistance for Law Enforcement Act (1994)
- Driver's Privacy Protection Act (1994)
- Health Insurance Portability and Accountability Act (HIPAA) (1996)
- Computer Fraud and Abuse Act (1996)
- Children's Online Privacy Protection Act (COPPA) (1998)
- Digital Millennium Copyright Act (1998)
- Gramm-Leach-Bliley Act (GLBA) (1999)
- USA PATRIOT Act (2001)
- Federal Information Security Management Act (2002)
- Fair and Accurate Credit Transactions Act (2003)
- CAN-SPAM Act (2003)
- 46 State Data Breach Disclosure Laws* law (2003-present).

*The U.S. Virgin Islands, Puerto Rico, and the District of Columbia have also enacted data breach disclosure laws.

This is not an exhaustive list, but it is representative and exemplifies the increasing growth in legislation. Given that information security and privacy are becoming more important, as evidenced by the growth in public policy, policy analysis in this area is timely and relevant.

Policy analysis aims to address questions such as the following. What do governments choose to do or not to do? How effective are the proposed or enacted solutions to public problems? How are issues that affect large numbers of citizens introduced to the public arena? What are the historical, political, and institutional factors that shape the formulation of public policy? In light of the relationships among policies, which of the various alternative policies will be most effective in achieving a given set of social goals? How can policymaking improve through research and analysis?

This chapter considers the data breach disclosure laws recently enacted in most of the United States. There are three important factors that make the state data breach disclosure laws of interest: the rapid policy growth; the first concrete example of informational regulation for information security; and the importance of these laws to prevent identity theft and protect privacy. The chapter begins with a discussion of the policy analysis framework used for this analysis. Thereafter, the chapter offers a retrospective analysis of the historical, political, and institutional factors that gave rise to these laws, i.e., the legislative outcomes seen today. Finally, the chapter concludes with suggestions for information security and privacy policy in the future.

INSTITUTIONAL ANALYSIS AND DEVELOPMENT FRAMEWORK

The institutional analysis and development (IAD) framework is a tool for performing policy analysis that focuses on how institutions, i.e., structures and mechanisms of social order, govern behavior. The goal of using this framework is to organize one's inquiry into a subject, which in this chapter are the data breach disclosure laws. The IAD framework is associated with the social theory of new institutionalism, which grew out of a desire to study institutions from a sociological perspective. Whereas old institutionalism studies formal institutions — such as organizations, norms, laws, and markets — new institutionalism adds the study of how institutions operate in a sociological context. In new institutionalism, institutions are abstractly defined as "shared concepts used by humans in repetitive situations organized by rules, norms and strategies." (Ostrom, 1999, p. 37) New institutionalism considers topics such as how individuals and groups construct institutions, how institutions function in practice, how institutions interact and affect each other, the effect that the sociological environment has on these interactions, and the effects of institutions on society. In new institutionalism, institutions are both the entities (organizations, laws, and markets) themselves, as well as things — rules, norms, and strategies — that shape the patterns of interaction across these entities.

While rules and norms are powerful, they are largely invisible, which makes identifying and measuring them difficult (Ostrom, 1999). One can describe them, but not precisely. This is important, since readers of this chapter will clearly see qualitative descriptions to depict institutions in action, but not quantitative measures. As a result, the description of this type, by its nature, includes connotation, which cannot be avoided; norms exist in us, not apart from us. Therefore, this chapter is subject to the author's bias. Readers must refute and/or improve upon this work. It is incumbent on all who are interested in such research to be aware of, and guard against, personal biases where they may limit findings.

The IAD framework appears in Figure 5-1. The action arena in the middle of the figure includes the action situations and the actors. In describing the action situation(s), the analyst attempts to identify the relevant structures, i.e., those affecting the process of interest. This can include participants; allowable actions, and linkages to outcomes; the level of control that participants have over choice; information available to participants; and costs and benefits assigned to actions and outcomes. The analyst also identifies the pertinent actors. Actors are individuals and groups (entities) who take action, i.e., they behave in a manner to which they attach meaning, either subjectively or instrumentally. Moving to the right in Figure 5-1, the IAD model includes patterns of interaction and outcomes. Most social reality includes multiple action arenas that interlink; some may say they are entangled. The IAD framework calls out patterns of interaction as subjects of interest in their own right as well as in relation to action situations and actors, and to outcomes. Outcomes are observed, inferred, and/or expected behaviors or results.

Moving to the left of the framework, action arenas can also be dependent variables. In this way, the analyst looks at how rules-in-use, attributes of community, and physical/material conditions influence the action arena. Rules-in-use are shared understandings about what is expected, required, and allowed in ordering relationships. Physical/material conditions refer to the characteristics of the states of the world as they shape action arenas. Clearly, what is expected or allowed may be conditioned by what is physically or materially possible. Likewise, physical conditions might shape rules-in-use and vice versa. Attributes of community are nonphysical conditions that provide structure to the community. Attributes of community may or may not be shaped by physical conditions and can serve to influence rules-in-use and the utilization of physical conditions. Moving right to left in the IAD model, one can also study how outcomes influence physical conditions, attributes of community, and rules-in-use. Consistent with the new institutional paradigm, the IAD model assumes that social systems are continually constituted and reconstituted; in this way, both the systems and the models to analyze them are organic in their worldview.

The IAD model does not prescribe how analysis is performed. The arrows do not mean to suggest that the analyst needs to work through the model in full, or from left to right. For example, an analyst can work from 1) the action arena to 2) outcomes in an effort to discern or predict patterns of interaction. Another alternative would be to work from 1) observed outcomes to 2) effects thereof on rules-in-use or attributes of community. Or the analyst can work across levels, e.g., investigating how collective choice rules-in-use such as excludability and the free-rider problem influence what type of operational policy can be enacted. This ability to study multiple aspects of an institution simultaneously is the power of this model. The IAD model is especially useful for analyzing self-governing entities; self-governing entities are comprised of individuals who create and influence the rules that structure their lives. In other words, the members (or their representatives) of a self-governing entity participate in the development of the collective-choice and constitutional rules-in-use. Self-governing entities are complex, adaptive systems in that they consist of a large number of elements interacting in multiple ways; the interactions change the system, which shapes future interactions such that outcomes are hard to predict, and thus, considered emergent. Self-governing entities are polycentric, in which citizens organize multiple governing authorities and private arrangements at different scales. A constitutional government is a self-governing entity; in an interesting contrast, the Internet is also a self-governing socio-technical entity. Public policy in information assurance and security is about how a polycentric system governs a polycentric system, making the IAD framework a useful analytic tool for this paper.

Retrospective Analysis.

The retrospective analysis examines rules-in-use, attributes of community, and the physical and material conditions that served to shape the policy actions we have seen to date in information security and privacy. Given that the data breach disclosure laws aim to ameliorate identity theft and privacy concerns, we start with an overview of other legislation in these areas.

Policy Actions to Date.

The first U.S. law that specifically addressed identity theft was passed in 1998 — the Identity Theft and Assumption Deterrence Act, passed in response to the dramatic rise in identity (ID) theft in the 1990s. Prior to this act, ID theft was not regulated per se. With regard to privacy, there is no provision for privacy in the U.S. Constitution. There is no independent privacy oversight agency in the United States, and the United States has no comprehensive privacy law. Instead, the United States has taken a sectorial approach to privacy regulation so that records held by third parties — such as financial and personal records at banks, educational and personal records at universities, membership and personal information at associations, and medical and personal records at community hospitals — are generally not protected unless a legislature has enacted a specific law. As a result, we have a patchwork of laws enacted to address privacy and data security. These are outlined next, starting with the laws that pertain to the federal government, followed by laws that pertain to the private sector, and finally, state laws.

Federal Laws.

The Federal Trade Commission (FTC) Act was established by the Federal Trade Commission in 1914 for the purposes of promoting consumer protection and eliminating and preventing anticompetitive business practices. Jurisdiction of the FTC Act extends to a variety of entities. Section 5 of the FTC Act forbids unfair or deceptive practices in commerce, where unfair practices are defined as those that cause or will likely cause substantial injury to consumers. Section 5 of the Federal Trade Commission Act has been used with regard to privacy and security, when companies have been accused of deceptive claims regarding use of personal information (e.g., Choicepoint). In 2003, the FTC Act was amended to include a provision regarding the privacy of consumers' credit data (the Fair and Accurate Transactions Act of 2003 - 15 U.S.C. 1681-1681x).

The Privacy Act of 1974 (5 U.S.C. 552a) governs the federal government's information privacy program. The intent of the Privacy Act is to balance the government's need to maintain information about individuals and the privacy rights of individuals. The Privacy Act protects individuals against unwarranted invasions of privacy stemming from federal agencies' collection, maintenance, use, and disclosure of personal information (U.S. Department of Justice, 2008). The U.S. Congress passed the act in response to revelations of privacy abuse during President Richard Nixon's administration. A second goal of the Privacy Act is to address potential abuses stemming from the government's increasing use of computers to store and retrieve personal data. The Privacy Act focuses on four basic policy objectives:

1. To restrict the disclosure of personally identifiable records maintained by federal agencies.

2. To grant individuals increased rights of access to federal agency records that pertain to themselves.

3. To grant individuals the right to seek amendment of federal agency records maintained on themselves, given evidence that the records are inaccurate, irrelevant, untimely, or incomplete.

4. To establish a code of "fair information practices" that requires federal agencies to comply with statutory norms regarding collection, maintenance, and dissemination of records.

The Privacy Act specifies that agencies will not disclose any record contained in a system of records by any means of communication to any person or to another agency without the prior written consent of the individual to whom the record pertains—barring exceptions such as law enforcement. The Privacy Act also mandates that each federal agency have in place an administrative and physical security system to prevent unauthorized release of personal records. While the Privacy Act also applies to records created by government contractors, it does not apply to private databases.

The Federal Information Security Management Act (44 U.S.C. 3544) (FISMA), enacted in 2002, is the principal law governing the information security program for the federal government. FISMA calls for agencies to develop, document, and implement agency-wide information security programs. This includes information systems used or operated by an agency or by a contractor of an agency. A goal of FISMA is to see that information security protections are commensurate with the risk and magnitude of harm resulting from unauthorized access, use, disclosure, disruption, modification, or destruction of information collected or maintained by or on behalf of the agency. FISMA requires procedures for detecting, reporting, and responding to security incidents. Notification of security incidents must be provided to a federal information security incident center, law enforcement, and relevant Offices of the Inspector General. The Office of Management and Budget Breach Notification Policy, issued in 2007, reemphasizes agencies' obligations under the Privacy Act and FISMA by outlining two new privacy requirements and five new security requirements, which include explicit requirements for breach notification.

The Veterans Affairs Information Security Act (38 U.S.C. 5722) was enacted in 2006 in response to the May 2006 breach of 26.5 million veterans' personal data. The Veterans Affairs Information Security Act requires the Veterans Administration (VA) to implement agency-wide information security procedures to protect the VA's sensitive personal information and information systems. While the VA Secretary must comply with FISMA, this act includes other requirements not in FISMA, which are not specified here due to the narrow scope of this law, i.e., it applies only to the VA.

Private Sector Laws.

In addition to the laws that shape the behavior of federal agencies, a suite of information security and privacy laws apply to the private sector. The two main laws are the Health Insurance Portability and Accountability Act (42 U.S.C. 1320) of 1996 (HIPAA) and the Gramm-Leach-Bliley Act (15 U.S.C. 6801-6809), enacted in 1999 (GLBA). HIPAA requires health plans, health care clearinghouses, and health care providers to ensure the privacy of medical records and prohibits disclosure without patient consent. While HIPAA includes privacy provisions, it is important to note that the primary purpose of HIPAA was job mobility. According to Hinde:

> It was perceived that the disclosure of pre-existing medical conditions or claims to a new employer and that employer's health plan might discourage job mobility if those conditions were excluded by the new health plan insurer. Thus, the concept of providing privacy over identifiable information for those covered by the plan (Hinde, 2003, p. 379).

The security standards that require health care entities to maintain administrative, technical, and physical safeguards to ensure the confidentiality, integrity, and availability of electronic "protected health information" were added to HIPAA in 2003 .

The Gramm-Leach-Bliley Act (GLBA) pertains to financial institutions. The impetus for GLBA was to "modernize" financial services. This included the removal of regulations that prevented the merger of banks, stock brokerage companies, and insurance companies. These financial institutions regularly bought and sold information that many would consider private, including bank balances and account numbers. Therefore, the:

> (R)emoval of these regulations raised significant risks that these new financial institutions would have ac-

cess to an incredible amount of personal information with no restrictions upon its use. Prior to GLBA, the insurance company that maintained your health records was distinct from the bank that mortgaged your house and the stockbroker that traded your stocks. Once these companies merged, however, they would have the ability to consolidate, analyze, and sell the personal details of their customers' lives (EPIC, 2008).

GLBA requires financial institutions—businesses that engage in banking, insuring, stocks and bonds, financial advice, and investing—to safeguard the security and confidentiality of customer information, to protect against threats and hazards to the security or integrity of these records, and to provide customers with notice of privacy policies. Section 501 (b) of GLBA requires banking agencies to establish industry standards regarding security measures such as risk assessment, information security training, security testing, monitoring, and a response program for unauthorized access to customer information and customer notice. In this way, GLBA is self-regulatory because it calls for financial institutions to appoint an intermediary to determine best practices for information security and to monitor the performance of financial institutions against these industry standards.

State Data Breach Disclosure Laws.

The most recent spate of activity is in the 46 state data breach disclosure laws. California was the first state to establish a data breach disclosure law in 2003; 10 other states enacted laws in 2005, 19 in 2006, eight in 2007, five in 2008, two in 2009, and one in 2010. Questions and concerns about the efficacy of these laws are many. All of these laws address three common elements: personal information definition, notification requirements, and notification procedures and timelines. However, the definitions of "personal information," "breach," "encryption," and "potential risk" are not consistent across the various state laws. This creates challenges for companies that operate in more than one state. The need to comply with multiple state laws can be cumbersome and costly. Thus far, it is not known if consumer notification is effective and under what circumstances. Given that the laws vary with regard to what is protected, to what degree, and when, consumer advocates fear that that lack of consistency diminishes the effectiveness of the laws. By allowing consumer rights to vary, consumers lose their power and, as a result of their protections meaning many different things, these consumer protections mean no one thing. Questions also arise about the use of personal notification as a mitigation strategy. As notifications increase, there is an increased risk of consumer desensitization, which ironically could cause consumers to be inattentive to the risk, which would be counterproductive.

The clarion call is that we are drowning under a myriad of different state data breach notification laws, thereby making a federal data breach notification law imperative. In response, 15 federal data breach notification bills have been introduced in the past 4 years. While all of these bills are dead, the discussion of preemptive federal law continues. The debate continues as to the needs of business versus consumer groups. As business vies for a high threshold for notification due to the fact that notification costs time, money, and reputation, consumer groups contend that higher thresholds do not grant enough notice to consumers. Questions of what *should be* with regard to identity theft, privacy, and security remain salient.

Retrospective Policy Analysis.

We now turn to a discussion of the policy analysis using the IAD framework to consider why and how we arrived at the development of the 46 existing data breach laws. In this retrospective analysis, we consider the rules-in-use, attributes of community, and the physical and material conditions that served to shape the policy actions we have seen until now. To date, public policy in information security and privacy in the United States has been largely incremental in nature. We can see from the patchwork of laws discussed earlier in this chapter that we have thus far resisted a coordinated federal law that preempts existing legislation. Incrementalism is common in self-governing, polycentric entities. In policy analysis, incrementalism assumes that: 1) the effects of seriality enhance outcomes by reducing uncertainty; and, 2) the enhanced consideration of context enhances outcomes. That the information age has introduced a number of uncertainties makes incrementalism especially relevant.

Stated more directly, and in connection to the IAD model, one of the rules-in-use is incrementalism. When there is a high degree of uncertainty, policy will be enacted incrementally. Thus, a plethora of laws is to be expected. While identity theft is nothing new, the magnitude of identity theft experienced in the past decade is new. The global information infrastructure is in its infancy — it is still unclear what people will and will not do in the electronic frontier. The Internet was never designed to serve the myriad of purposes for which it is being used, nor was it designed for billions of users. Laws designed in the industrial era may or may not apply in the information age. It is not certain what new laws are necessary as a result of information technologies and how effective these laws will be.

During this period of transition, new communities form and existing communities are being reshaped; as a result, behavioral norms are being renegotiated. Given the global nature of the Internet, it is reasonable to view these communities as more heterogeneous or, at a minimum, heterogeneous in new ways. Therefore, norms cannot be easily transported based on existing communities; they will have to be established from the ground up, which is bound to take time. Additionally, because the technology is still new, scientists and engineers are still determining what actions are physically possible. Talented individuals around the world are working on technologies to help anonymize data, enhance privacy-preserving computation, and provide improved intrusion detection, but this takes time as well. Experience in all of these areas — rules-in-use, attributes of community, and physical/material conditions — occur through observation, involvement, and exposure.

Though we do not have much experience, there has been the need to take action. ID theft is on the rise, which concerns citizens. Two of the core imperatives of the state are domestic order and legitimacy (Dryzek, Downes, Hunold, Schlosberg and Hernes, 2003). Yet, the existing federal and private sector laws are not sufficient to address the rising identity theft problem threatening domestic order, thereby forcing lawmakers to take action to ensure their perceived legitimacy. In response, federal laws have been amended, private sector laws are being tweaked, and a flurry of state laws have been enacted. To what can we attribute the incremental changes we have observed? Why do we have these laws as opposed to something else? To answer these questions, we turn to a discussion of openness and transparency, informational regulation, the infancy of the information industry, and federalism; we further examine how rules-in-use, attributes of community, and physical/material conditions have intersected in each of these areas to produce the policies we have today.

Openness and Transparency.

A democracy is founded on principles of openness and transparency. In 1933, Justice Louis D. Brandeis coined the powerful phrase "sunlight as disinfectant" in support of increasing openness and transparency in public policy. While laws that aim to ensure openness and transparency in government operations existed before 1933, Brandeis is responsible for the term "Sunshine Laws." The impetus behind sunshine laws is twofold. First, a thriving, open democracy depends on open access and citizen participation; thus, the right-to-know is a constitutional and inherent right of American citizens. Second, a government that is of the people, for the people, and by the people asserts government subservience to the individual, which predicates freedom of information.

The Freedom of Information Act (FOIA), signed into law on July 4, 1966, by President Lyndon B. Johnson, is a Sunshine Law. FOIA allows for the full or partial disclosure of previously unreleased information and documents controlled by the U.S. Government. The concept of "freedom of information" conveys a philosophy that values the advantages of increasing our ability to gather and send information, and clearly does not connote privacy as a positive right. This acts as a rule-in-use.

The Privacy Act of 1974 arrived 8 years later as an amendment to the FOIA in response to Watergate and the abuse of privacy during the Nixon administration.

The Privacy Act of 1974 did not promote privacy, but established a code of fair information practice. It was also an attempt to limit the powers of government and passed hastily during the final week of the 93rd Congress, which was in session from 1973-74. According to the U.S. Department of Justice:

> [N]o conference committee was convened to reconcile differences in the bills passed by the House and Senate. Instead, staffs of the respective committees—led by Senators Ervin and Percy, and Congressmen Moorhead and Erlenborn—prepared a final version of the bill that was ultimately enacted . . . the Act's imprecise language, limited legislative history, and somewhat outdated regulatory guidelines have rendered it a difficult statute to decipher and apply (U.S. Department of Justice, 2008).

Moreover, even after more than 25 years of administrative and judicial analysis, numerous Privacy Act issues remain unresolved or unexplored. Adding to these interpretational difficulties is the fact that many Privacy Act cases are unpublished district court decisions.

This offers important insight into the historical context with regard to how information and privacy are embedded in the past as well as food for thought on how this norm has shaped our ongoing collective treatment of it going forward. Through the enactment of FOIA in 1966, the push to enable information sharing was a result of mistrust in government. Eight years later, the Privacy Act was reactive in nature and reflective of further distrust of government. Through these pieces of legislation run two noteworthy threads. First is the value of freedom of information, wherein information belongs to and exists for the advancement of citizens and the common good. Second is a distrust of government powers, wherein stewardship cannot be entrusted to the polity. "Privacy" in the Privacy Act is not a positive right, but rather a necessary provision subservient to limiting government powers.

Earlier in this study it was noted that HIPAA was passed to enable job mobility and GLBA was passed to modernize the financial services industry. Again, in the context of these laws, privacy is secondary to another purpose. In HIPAA and GLBA, privacy is a means to an end; in other words, privacy plays a functional or instrumental role. Society needs privacy because citizens need job mobility; society needs privacy to modernize financial services. Implicit is the message that if citizens did not need job mobility or financial services modernization they would not need to concern themselves with privacy. Even though privacy was cast as a functional need in both HIPAA and GLBA, the similarity ends there. These industry sectors have significantly different regulatory frameworks (Congressional Research Service, 2008). The security and privacy provisions in these laws are more reflective of the larger regulatory framework for these industries. The regulatory framework for these industries served as additional rules-in-use, shaping these laws.

Informational Regulation.

Another phenomenon that is essential to understanding the U.S. data breach laws is informational regulation. Informational regulation has become a striking development in American law (Sunstein, 2006). To date, informational regulation has applied in the environmental and health policy arenas. It is noteworthy that informational regulation has been applied to these areas. In the case of environmental policy, informational regulations have protected aspects of the environment that are common (or public) good in nature, which by definition means that the private sector will not attend to them. A similar situation occurs in the area of public health, in which the health of all citizens is both good for the individual as well as for the collective as a means and an end, i.e., it is a common or public good.

Informational regulation has two functions. First, it serves to inform people of potential risk exposure (Volokh, 2002) and serves as "sunlight," which was already discussed as the value of transparency. Second, informational regulation aims to change the behavior of risk creators (Volokh, 2002) and to exert pressure on entities to care for the common good. Informational regulation is useful in a polycentric policy arena in which the problems that the policy means to address are attributable to multiple sources, the solutions require participation from multiple parties, and the nature of problems and solutions is dynamic—all of which necessitate that the policy must allow for adaptability. Clearly caring for the environment or health are polycentric policy areas. Environmental and health problems stem from multiple sources, and ameliorating these types of problems takes ongoing involvement from multiple parties. The same is true for data security, identity protection, and privacy. Improved data security is possible only under conditions that shape the practices of numerous individuals and covered entities; therefore, policy that provides incentives for such change is, in theory, necessary. How does informational regulation work in practice?

Figure 5-2 shows the mechanistic view of the premise for informational regulation for data breach disclosure laws. Informational regulation intends to provide warning information to consumers. In theory, by enhancing the knowledge level, consumers can perform a personalized risk assessment and make purchase decisions based on that assessment. The market decisions made by consumers intend to drive the less secure entities out of the market, thereby improving the state of security overtime. In addition, the enhanced knowledge levels will propel consumers to engage in other protective actions, such as active credit monitoring or a credit freeze. Consumer credit monitoring typically includes alerting the bank and credit card merchant, notifying the FTC, and/or contacting law enforcement. A credit freeze allows consumers to lock their consumer credit report and scores. Once consumers have locked their credit information, the lender or merchant cannot access it, which significantly lowers the likelihood that the merchant will issue credit. The benefit is that the thief is not likely to get credit in the consumer's name (so the law prevents a false-positive, also called a Type II error). The downside is that this locking also impedes consumers from quickly getting credit in their name (a false-negative, or Type I error); note that consumers can release the freeze, but it takes a few days and may jeopardize quick access to special loans and other purchase incentives. These proactive consumer measures will in theory also lead to improved security over time.

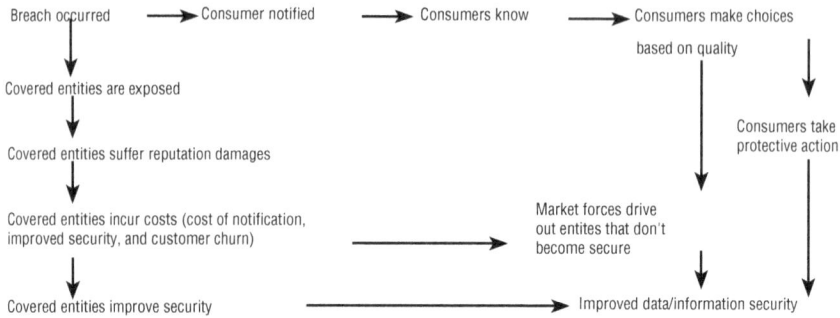

**Figure 5-2. Informational Regulation Premise
for Data Breach Disclosure Laws.**

Informational regulation also aims to change the actions of producers. By engaging producers in providing information, informational regulation, in theory, reveals an entity's practices. This sends a signal to society that perhaps this entity cannot be trusted. The premise is that covered entities value their reputations. As such, they will act to improve their security in order to preserve their reputations and minimize associated costs, which could include the costs of the notification itself, as well as downtime costs, the costs of remediation and recovery due to the breach, and the costs of lost business. Ideally, these two streams combine to improve data security, which in turn mitigates ID theft and enhanced privacy.

The premise of informational regulation is that: 1) market mechanisms can shape risk behavior, thereby reducing the need for command-and-control regulations; and, 2) informational regulation enhances democratic processes and promotes individual autonomy. By providing data breach information to victims, individuals are empowered to make decisions based on quality (i.e., they can elect to purchase goods/services from a provider who offers enhanced information security and privacy), and market mechanisms will be fortified. A failure to provide complete and accurate market information can impede the efficient allocation of goods and services and result in market failure, which is the driver for changing producers' behavior.

In theory, informational regulation allows more public monitoring of decisions, a norm already discussed. By forcing disclosure, more people are informed; and by informing more people, the quality and the quantity of public deliberation will improve, thereby enhancing the democratic processes that are vital for openness and transparency. In general, information disclosure rests on the normative belief that citizens have a right to know the risks to which they are exposed. This information promotes choice and autonomy, both of which are foundational to what some may consider the penultimate norm in American society — liberty (Renshaw, 2002).

In contrast to command-and-control regulation in which the government sets and enforces standards, informational regulation is often less expensive. The United States values efficient government, and recent decades have seen an increased emphasis on downsizing the federal government. While it is not clear that command and control legislation would be effective in mitigating data breaches or in making data breach disclosure more effective, it is clear that a command and control approach is not politically efficacious at this point in time.

In summary, informational regulation has grown in areas where consumer protection, private sector practices, and risk converge. Examples include warning labels regarding mercury levels, nutrition labels disclosing fat content, and notifications about the side effects of a given medication. That data security shares these same material features—consumer protection, private sector practices, and risk—has clearly contributed to adopting informational regulation as the model for data breach disclosure laws.

Infancy of the Information Industry and Federalism.

Continuing with a thread that was started earlier—relative inexperience with the information age—the information industry includes: 1) industries that buy and sell information as a good or service; 2) certain service sectors that are especially information intensive, such as banking and legal services; 3) information dissemination sectors, such as telecommunications and broadcasting; and, 4) producers of information processing devices, such as computers and software. The information industry is a boon to the economy, as information amplifies growth in more traditional industry sectors, and the demand for information goods and services increases markedly. Because of the ends and means nature of information goods and services, the market is quite large and still emerging.

An example of emergence is the following relatively recent cascade of events: the Internet explosion; September 11, 2001; and the subsequent war on terror. These events converged to boost the data brokerage industry. Data brokerages are companies that collect and sell billions of private and public records containing individuals' personal information. Many of these companies also provide products and services, including identity verification, background screening, risk assessments, individual digital dossiers, and tools for analyzing data. Most data brokers sell data that they collect from public records (e.g., driver's license records, vehicle registration records, criminal records, voter registration records, property records, and occupational licensing records) or from warranty cards, credit applications, etc. In addition, data brokers purchase so-called "credit headers" from credit reporting agencies. Information on a credit header generally includes a person's Social Security number, address, phone numbers, and birth date (Congressional Research Service, 2007). Although some of the products and services provided by data brokers are currently subject to privacy and security protections aimed at credit reporting agencies and the financial industry under the Fair Credit Reporting Act (1971) and GLBA (1999), many are not. Because the industry is relatively young, there is no history of oversight or self-regulation of the industry's practices, including the accuracy and handling of sensitive data, by an industry-sanctioned body.

Data brokerages are not the only unregulated entities. There are many other organizations that process, store, and transmit personal information: state and local agencies, public hospitals, departments of revenue and motor vehicles, courts at the state and local level, agencies that oversee elections, K-12 schools, school districts, post-secondary institutions, and business entities engaging in inter- and intrastate commerce. Most of these entities are not covered by HIPAA and GLBA (Congressional Budget Office, 2006) and have traditionally been governed through state law; hence, the 46 state data breach laws discussed earlier. The suite of laws are in part a result of lack of experience with information markets, and are partly a function of the need for legislation that spans the numerous and varied types of entities that process, store, and transmit personal information. A broad and amorphous social challenge such as information security and privacy is not only diffuse; it is emergent. Research has shown that in cases of open access, common good resources (such as security and privacy), collective choice action arenas, i.e., those that improve opportunities for communication and public deliberation, result in better joint outcomes (Ostrom, 1999). The patchwork of data breach laws fit this profile—they aim to increase communication and public deliberation.

In a federalist system, such as the United States, sovereignty is constitutionally divided between the federal government and the constituent states. The powers granted to the U.S. federal government are limited to the right to levy taxes, declare war, and regulate interstate and foreign commerce. The powers traditionally reserved by the states include public safety, public education, public health, transportation, and infrastructure. Of course, information security and privacy challenges permeate these state-governed organizations, too. While a federal preemptive law might span all organizations and individuals, there is the possibility that it would erode state sovereignty and, in the process, alter the federal-state balance of power in unprecedented ways. The patchwork suite of laws that we have can be partially attributed to a collective belief that this is wrong. This retrospective analysis provided nuanced insight into the present. Federal laws were enacted to delimit government powers, and privacy seemed necessary for that purpose. Private industry sector laws were passed to protect the private sector, and data security and privacy were functional means to that end. These federal and private sector laws reflect a general U.S. cultural norm of distrusting government while trusting in the private sector and market forces. Informational regulation was established as a form of legislation considered effective for issues that spanned consumer protection and risk, and where market mechanisms would/could work effectively, which is further evidence of pervasive trust in the private sector.

LOOKING FORWARD

Technological advancements are changing the information security and privacy landscape considerably; in response, organizations grapple to enact social controls, i.e., public policies, that mitigate the ill effects. Yet, these policies are blunt instruments not suited to the careful excision of these ills. As mentioned earlier, some critics contend that the nation is drowning under a myriad of different state data breach notification laws and argue for a preemptive federal data breach notification law. Others contend that the current laws can suffice if modifications are passed.

Some advocates of modifying existing laws assert that the outcome of data breach disclosure should be to motivate large-scale reporting so that data breaches and trends can be aggregated, which allows a more purposeful and defensive use of incident data. Those who advocate for large-scale data collection view the existing laws as "disclosure disincentives" for two reasons: 1) breached entities view themselves as victims of attack and not deserving of reputational repercussions; and, 2) existing laws offer covered entities considerable discretion as to whether to disclose. Together, these factors result in underreporting of data breaches, which in turn constrains large-scale data collection regarding breaches. The proposed policy solution is to modify the laws to make breach notification completely anonymous where breached entities report to an intermediary and not to consumers.

Whereas others who advocate for modifying the existing laws suggest coordinated response architecture (CRA) (Schwartz and Janger, 2007), supporters of this alternative agree that large-scale data collection on data breaches is necessary, but contend that consumer notification needs to be amended, not eliminated. Their main concerns with the existing consumer notification practices are that: 1) there are too many notifications, leading to consumer desensitization; and, 2) the information provided to consumers is unhelpful at best and befuddling at worst. In response, this group advocates for amendments to the data breach laws to include a CRA. The CRA is an intermediary agency with responsibility for: 1) supervised delegation of the decision whether to give notice; 2) coordination and targeting of notices to other institutions and to customers; and, 3) improving the content of notices sent to consumers.

Each of the alternatives offers a critique of the existing suite of laws. Each critique is grounded in a premise of what outcomes matter, and each alternative offers a view on how policy can/should target actions in pursuit of these outcomes. Questions of what should be with regard to ID theft, privacy, and security remain salient. The problem is both highly polycentric and emergent, and these conditions favor polycentric and incremental policy approaches.

Yet, others would suggest that informational regulation is the wrong type of legislation entirely, and that tort law would be more effective for redressing problems of negligent behavior. Still others support a mix-and-match set of policy alternatives. One example is a preemptive federal law in conjunction with tort laws and existing state laws, in which the scope of preemption is fairly narrow. The justification is that such a policy mix would allow greater stringency, and therein sovereignty, in state laws as desired by states, but provide for certain requirements in a federal law in areas that are crucial to improving security.

As opposed to thinking about discrete policy solutions, challenges in information security and privacy are highly polycentric and emergent; these conditions in turn favor polycentric and incremental policy approaches. The 46 state data breach laws put data security into the hands of citizens and organizations. In a society pillared by equity and freedom as ideals, where there is no constitutional provision for privacy, the constant for deliberating the common good is through an open and representative process. This myriad of data security laws aim to serve the purpose of making explicit these individual preferences in a manner that allows all to translate these preferences into collective choice—the future of data security is contingent on seeing more laws enacted to address facets of information security and privacy, and second, that these laws are likely to be more polycentric, not less.

REFERENCES

Congressional Budget Office, (2006). *CBO S. 1789 Personal data privacy and security act of 2005 cost estimate.* Available from *www.cbo.gov/doc.cfm?index=7161.*

Congressional Research Service, (2007). "Data Brokers: Background and Industry Overview," *CRS Report for Congress RS22137-070112.* Available from *opencrs.com/.*

Congressional Research Service, (2008). "Federal Information Security and Data Breach Notification Laws," *CRS Report for Congress RS33199.* Available from *opencrs.com/.*

Dark, Melissa J., ed. "Information Assurance and Security Ethics in Complex Systems: Interdisplinary Perspectives," Hershey, PA: IGI Global. Available from *www.igi-global.com.*

Dryzek, J., D. Downes, C. Hunold, D. Schlosberg, and H. Hernes. (2003). *Green States and Social Movements.* New York: Oxford University Press.

Electronic Privacy Information Center (EPIC), (2008). *The Graham-Leach-Bliley Act.* Available from *epic.org/privacy/glba/.*

Fair Credit Reporting Act, at 15 U.S.C. § 1681 (1971).

Federal Trade Commission Act, 15 U.S.C. § 41-58 (1914).

GovTrack.us . Available from *www.govtrack.us/congress/bill*.

Health Insurance Portability and Accountability Act, 42 U.S.C. § 1320 (1996).

Hinde, S. (2003). Privacy legislation: A Comparison of the U.S. and European Approaches. *Computers and Security*, Vol. 22, No. 5, pp. 378-387.

Identity Theft Resource Center, (2008). Available from *www.idtheftcenter.org*.

Ostrom, E. (1999). Institutional Rational Choice. An assessment of the Institutional Analysis and Development Framework. In P. Sabatier, ed., *Theories of the Policy Process*, Boulder, CO: Westview Press, pp. 35-67.

Ostrom, E. (1990). *Governing the Commons: The Evolution of Institutions for Collective Action*. New York: Cambridge University Press.

Personal Data Security and Privacy Act of 2009, S. 1490, 111th Congress (2009).

Privacy Rights Clearinghouse (2008). *A Chronology of Data Breaches*. Available from *www.privacyrights.org/ar/ChronDataBreaches.htm#1*.

Renshaw, K. (2002). "Sounding Alarms: Does Informational Regulation Help or Hinder Environmentalism? *Environmental Law, 14*(3), pp. 654-697.

Schwarz, P. and E. Janger (2007). "Notification of Data Breaches," *Michigan Law Review,* Vol. 105, p. 913.

Sunstein, C. (1999). Informational Regulation and Information Standing: Atkins and Beyond. *University of Pennsylvania Law Review*, Vol. 147, No. 3, pp. 613-675.

U.S. Department of Justice, (2008). Available from *www.usdoj.gov/oip/04_7_1.html*.

Veterans Affairs Information Security Act, 38 U.S.C. § 5722 (2006).

Volokh, A. (2002). The Pitfalls of the Environmental Right-to-Know, *2002 Utah Law Review*, pp. 805-841.

CHAPTER 6

CYBER SECURITY AND IDENTITY: SOLUTIONS FOR CRITICIAL INFRASTRUCUTURE THAT PROTECT CIVIL LIBERTIES AND ENHANCE SECURITY

Joshua Gruenspecht

INTRODUCTION: IDENTITY PROBLEMS AND IDENTITY VALUES

Problems with identity determination raise some of the most complicated and unresolved issues in cyber security. Just as in the physical world, identity online can be crucial both in restricting access to critical resources and in responding appropriately to threats or attacks. In the networked world, however, identifying a communications partner can be difficult, and information security can suffer as a result. Industry and government are pursuing a number of approaches to better identify communicants so as to secure information and other assets. As part of this process, some policymakers have suggested fundamental changes to the way in which the Internet transmits identity information. Though their solutions have varied, this subset of policymakers has coalesced around the general idea that Internet communication needs to be more traceable so that malefactors can be tracked more easily.

What these policymakers often fail to recognize is that identity is bigger than cyber security alone. Changes to online identity standards may also have effects on civil liberties and global freedom, economic and technological innovation, market choices, consumer privacy, and other issues associated with online business models. Authentication mechanisms that do not consider commercial compatibility may be left behind in the marketplace, while enforced compatibility may create barriers to entry for entrepreneurs. Mechanisms mandated by the government, though, may choke off superior private-sector solutions. Enhanced identity mechanisms may complicate the right to anonymous speech and increase the ability of repressive regimes to target dissenters. In all these ways, network identity is not just a matter of security, but also a matter of civil and economic freedom. Accordingly, the development and implementation of identity solutions must involve a weighing of values.[1] Increasing the traceability of communications endangers many of these values. Instead of expending limited resources to pursue solutions that have serious negative consequences, it is incumbent upon policymakers to first consider alternative ways to address the cyber security identity problem.

In order to assess the full spectrum of identity solutions proposed for cyber security, it is useful to understand that there are two related but distinct sets of problems in network identification: authentication and attribution. Authentication refers to the process of verifying the identity of a communicant (a machine or a user). Where an identity is associated with certain permissions, authentication mechanisms can be used to protect critical resources by securing systems from unauthorized access. Attribution, in contrast, concerns questions of how to determine the identity of a communicant (as the source of certain code or other data) based on all of the information that the communicant has placed onto the network, including metadata associated with his or her communications. Attribution strategies can help assign responsibility for an attack. They can also help identify threats to network security, thus helping to mitigate those threats before their impact is felt. In some scenarios, authentication information can play a significant role in attribution, though often policymakers gloss over this piece of the attribution equation.

The first section considers both sets of problems and concludes that authentication-oriented solutions are more likely to provide significant security benefits and less likely to produce undesirable economic and civil liberties consequences. The second section explains the concepts of authentication and attribution in greater depth, discussing how each relates to network security and to other core values. The third section explains how identity information is currently exchanged on the Internet, and what authentication and attribution challenges are raised by these existing solutions. The fourth section evaluates proposed solutions to identity problems and the policy issues associated with those solutions, explaining the benefits and drawbacks of each for both cyber security and for other values. The last section provides conclusions reached as a result of this analysis.

AUTHENTICATION AND ATTRIBUTION: IDENTIFYING THE COMMUNICANT

Authentication: Demanding Identity Before a Transaction.

Authentication is "the process of establishing an understood level of confidence that an identifier refers to a particular individual or identity."[2] Authentication often involves an exchange of information before some other transaction in order to ensure — to the extent necessary for the transaction at hand — that the sender of a stream of traffic is who he or she claims to be or otherwise has the attributes required to engage in the given transaction.[3] Enhancing the security of the authentication process in turn enhances the security of the transaction. Because critical resources such as utility control systems, financial networks, and systems holding classified information are increasingly accessible through the Internet, authenticating users becomes an important cyber security concern. There are two sets of authentication questions that drive security. First, how can authentication security be improved? Second, what level of authentication should be required in any particular situation?

To understand how improvements happen, it is important to understand the underlying authentication transaction. There are three parties to an authentication transaction.[4] The "user" associates him or herself with a digital identity; the "identity provider" facilitates and stores that association; and the "relying party" asks the identity provider to verify the user at the time of the transaction (or relies on something provided to the user by the identity provider). In many situations, the identity provider and the relying party are one and the same (e.g., a business issuing user names and passwords for access to its own internal network, or Google authenticating a user into Gmail). Combining the two can increase security by reducing both the number of parties to the transaction and the technological complexity of the transaction, but it can also reduce security because, when every relying party issues it own identities, users (even sophisticated ones at important facilities) engage in insecure practices.[5]

Information exchanged to authenticate identity is often broken down into three separate classes of authenticators: something you know, such as a password; something you have, such as a card or USB token; and something you are, such as biometric information.[6] Including multiple factors, especially from different classes, generally increases the security of the transaction.

Creating a digital identity generally requires some form of "proofing," a pre-authentication step in which the user and the identity provider exchange other authenticators. This process sometimes involves off-line identities and sometimes involves, especially for higher levels of security, an in-person interaction. If the authenticators used to prove identity are themselves invalid, or the proofing process is otherwise inadequate, the resulting identity credentials will not be reliable.

Underlying the second question, "What level of authentication should be required?" is the supposition that different kinds of transactions should require different levels of authentication. Some observers believe that certain online transactions, for example, accessing a publicly available government website, can be permitted with no authentication, while others propose that at least some identification should be part of every Internet transaction.[7] Although, almost all technical solutions and policy proposals involving identity are based on the creation of levels of assurance (LOAs).[8] LOAs rank networked systems according to the consequences of authentication failure and define authentication requirements at each level. Accessing a newspaper article, for example, surely requires fewer assurances of identity than accessing the control system of a nuclear reactor. Work has already been done to define LOAs for federal systems,[9] and private sector identity initiatives have followed the government's four-level framework.[10] However, what is lacking, certainly in the private sector, is any agreement on what level of assurance is required for what type of transaction or access. To the extent that this lack of agreement leaves critical resources inadequately protected raises significant cyber security concerns as to why there has been a failure to adopt standard LOAs.

To some degree, cyber security identity may benefit from developments in the e-commerce and social networking sectors, where identity and authentication are hot topics. Online service providers recognize that users dislike the complexity of maintaining multiple identities, and therefore providers want to streamline their identity processes. At the same time, advertisers and advertising platforms see huge benefit from linking online activity with offline or true name identity.[11] As a result, multiparty efforts are underway to create identification systems that will work across sites,[12] and individual companies such as Facebook are stepping forward as universal commercial identity providers.[13] Combining these efforts with cyber security efforts might have beneficial network effects such as the reduction of complexity. However, these commercial solutions are not likely to have the proofing mechanisms or implementation security required to serve at high LOAs.

Finally, authentication solution designers in the commercial context have to take into account user expectations, since users may abandon services that fail to protect anonymity when users consider it integral to their use of the service.[14] Attempts to apply cyber security authentication solutions at lower LOAs may face similar resistance.[15]

Attribution: Determining Identity after a Transaction.

Attribution is the analysis of information associated with a transaction or series of transactions to try to determine the identity of a sender of a stream of traffic. Information collection and analysis is the focus of attribution. Transaction design is also relevant to the extent that it can help assure the availability of information to analyze.

The absence of an easy means of identifying the originator of malicious traffic gives rise to security policy concerns at multiple levels.[16] First, on a practical level, the recipient of unwanted traffic is more limited in its ability to respond to the problem if it cannot identify the sender of that traffic. That recipient may restrict further traffic from a given network source, for example, but will have to regroup if the sender re-routes his or her traffic. Second, as a matter of tort and criminal law, it is difficult to construct a legal case against a virtual interloper without attribution.

Third, as a matter of international law, the laws of war demand both proportionality of response and minimization of damage to the property of non-aggressors and neutral third parties. Even if there were a legal understanding of what actions constituted "cyber war," the use of military force would be impermissible under international law without the ability to determine the identity of the aggressor. Relatedly, an attribution deficit reduces the effectiveness of deterrence as a policy for discouraging bad actors, whether criminal or governmental. American foreign policy relies heavily on deterrence in other warfighting spaces. In cyberspace, a lack of attribution may handicap that reliance.[17]

Because attribution is a forensic discipline, the key problems revolve around the availability, collection, and analysis of information. There are multiple kinds of relevant information. Both the malicious code itself and associated communications metadata can offer hints as to the identity of the sender. Traffic routing information can help trace communications back to their starting point. Background intelligence can help contextualize transactional information.

Traffic routing information is particularly important to attribution. Meticulous attention to content can often remove traces of identity, but no sender can escape the fundamental truth of routing: content has to be sent from somewhere. As we discuss below, Internet protocol (IP) addresses are a useful source of identity information. However, some policymakers argue that Internet transactions do not offer enough information about routing and that changes in routing systems and/or networks must produce additional information for attribution.[18] Other experts warn, however, that network-level personal attribution is of limited forensic value. David D. Clarke and Susan Landau, for example, argue that, rather than issuing calls for better attribution on the network, applications should be designed that do a better job of integrating identity and attribution when and only when it is actually necessary.[19]

Increasing the ease of attribution may have unintended consequences. Re-engineering traffic routing for all Internet transactions will challenge privacy and anonymity, including in situations in which privacy and anonymity are in the best interests of the United States and other democratic countries.[20] In contrast, some regimes have demonstrated an interest in using Internet attribution as a means of controlling dissidents' access to information online.[21] In addition, if attribution solutions require Internet service providers to invest more heavily in specialized hardware or software, they may indirectly raise barriers to entry for new Internet services. Increasing attribution may also substantially affect policy efforts aimed at giving consumers greater control over the compilation of online profiles.[22] Weighing these consequences against the cyber security benefits is a critical task for policymakers.

Authorization and Auditing: Security Issues beyond Authentication and Attribution.

Although this chapter focuses on authentication and attribution, two other issues closely relate to identity and are critical elements of any secure system: authorization and auditing. Authorization is the process by which a given authenticated user identity is associated with a set of permissions. Authorization mechanisms are used, for example, to prevent the use of low-security accounts to access high-security information and controls. Policy interventions aimed at improving the technical security of authentication should not ignore the security of authorization mechanisms. Indeed, measures to improve authorization may offer some of the greatest benefits to cyber security at the least cost to other values.

Auditing, meanwhile, refers to two processes. The first consists of reviewing a system periodically to ensure that it continues to function properly. The second consists of reviewing a system after it fails to determine what caused that failure. Keeping adequate system logs and reviewing such logs regularly and thoroughly is a critical security function. Unless systems are audited, many compromises will never be discovered or will not be discovered until it is too late.

Though both authorization and auditing are important, authentication and attribution pose especially thorny policy questions and have been the focus of much recent debate. Accordingly, this chapter focuses on authentication and attribution as the key policy problems, although further examination of authorization and auditing is certainly justified.

IDENTITY AND THE INTERNET: HOW AUTHENTICATION AND ATTRIBUTION WORK IN PRACTICE, AND WHAT CONCERNS CURRENT SOLUTIONS RAISE

Identity on the Internet: How Parties Exchange Identity Information, and What Information They Exchange.

The Internet is a physical network of interconnected hardware devices. Each device uses the same suite of protocols, including the IP, to communicate. To forward data, the network of data connections between those physical devices relies on IP addresses — "logical" addresses — rather than any information about physical device type or location. This offers several benefits. One is that the individual networks that make up the Internet can interoperate without each one having to maintain an exhaustive list of the physical location of every communications partner on the Internet. Instead, routing protocols allow networks to determine which logical neighbor is closest to the destination, and to pass data along to that device. Not until the last step does the recipient's physical location matter. Another benefit is that physical devices of all kinds can join the Internet without having to adhere to a particular hardware specification. As long as a device can run the protocols, it can exchange data with other devices.

IP addresses are a key source of identity information exchanged with every Internet packet. As IP addresses are logical, not physical, they are not permanently tied to any particular user or machine. However, they do provide useful identity signifiers. Blocks of addresses are generally assigned to businesses and Internet service providers (ISPs) and then leased to individual users.[23] On its own, an IP address can often identify the country of origin and, depending on how the owner of a block assigns addresses, perhaps a region, a city or neighborhood, or even a particular location. Moreover, at any given moment, every IP address in use is known by the ISP to be linked to a particular device or a particular physical address, which can be determined with the cooperation of the Internet service provider. Though the ISP may not always be able to map an IP address directly to an end-user device (e.g., when a user is connecting through a wireless router), it can point an investigator in the right direction. As a result, IP addresses can be very useful in locating the origin of traffic.

The IP suite also requires that additional routing information be exchanged in Internet transactions. While this information does not relate directly to the identity of the transaction partners, it can be indirectly useful in identifying a sender. For example, packets contain a "time to live" (TTL) field, which counts down the number of routing hops that the packet has taken from source to destination. The TTL field can sometimes be useful in helping to determine how distant the originator of a given stream of traffic is from his or her target.

The last type of information contained within almost all Internet packets is content, which can also be useful in attribution. Individual packets of information may bear hallmarks of their origin or traces of data from their sender. Natural language contents may be written in a particular foreign language or show evidence of having been written using a language-specific keyboard layout. Exploits and other forms of malicious code may contain stylistic signatures associated with a particular user or group. Analysis of such content, however, is inevitably ad hoc.

Aside from these general sources of identifying information available within all Internet traffic streams, there are also information sources specific to authenticated transactions. For example, many online services require their users to authenticate themselves, which often provides a reliable means of identifying communicants. Generally, commercial services design their own authentication protocols. Given the many classes of services that require authentication—financial institutions, merchants, and so on—there are many different authentication protocols. The most common authentication paradigm for services involves setting up an encrypted connection to the user using a one-time key, requesting authenticators[24] from that user to establish identity, and then allowing the authenticated user access to the service.

Authentication may be performed by a third party (the issuing party), with credentials subsequently passed to the service provider (the relying party), or the service provider may perform the authentication itself.[25] In the first case (the "triangle model"), the relying party redirects the user login to the issuing party, which authenticates the user and then returns a token establishing the user's credentials to use the service provider site. One example of the triangle model is Facebook Connect, a service allowing users to leverage their Facebook identifications (IDs) to log into other sites. More sophisticated issuing parties may even handle authorization, returning a token that not only authenticates, but also specifies which services a user may use. In the second case, the service provider handles the authentication and authorization directly. An example of this bilateral model would be Apple's web services, which require that users establish accounts directly with Apple, and then authenticate directly to Apple itself.

Entities that rely on identities issued by others possess the local account ID of the user—perhaps a real name, perhaps not—but not information about additional authenticators, such as passwords or information obtained through proofing. The issuing party possesses that latter information. Service providers who use the bilateral model have all the information collected during both the initial proofing step and the authentication step.

Cyber Security Concerns: Problems with Existing Exchanges and Areas of Possible Policy Intervention.

Authentication Concerns.

Critical infrastructure is lagging in the adoption of secure authentication,[26] but this does not seem to be due to any technological issues. There appears to be general consensus that the available technological means of authentication are sufficiently secure to protect information.[27] Under that assumption, then, the most important policy issues in authentication are ensuring that, first, critical infrastructure appropriately adopts these technologies and, second, that critical infrastructure authorities properly implement these technologies to minimize the possibility of compromise from human error. Adoption within critical infrastructure may be slowed by the lack of product metrics, the absence of agreement on what level of assurance is appropriate for a given context, the dearth of information about cyber security risks and their costs, and poorly designed incentives for the adoption of improvements. Fundamental ease-of-use problems with identity technologies also exist, which may require additional innovation.

One barrier to adoption may be the absence of metrics surrounding the use of authentication technologies. The average system administrator may not understand the relative merits of one technology or product over another. Product metrics that made comparison across technologies or products simpler could improve the ability of information technology (IT) professionals to understand tradeoffs.

A second adoption barrier may be the absence of recognized levels of assurance for any given level of access or permission. Does a utility control system require more protection than a bank? Do different banking systems or functions require different levels of protection? If businesses knew which LOA was appropriate for a given system or function, they would have a common language with which to decide what level of security is appropriate. In turn, those levels of assurance can help make the creation of metrics easier as well, by allowing product security ratings to refer to LOAs.[28] To address these concerns, further work could be done to define appropriate LOAs for different private sector systems. In particular, LOAs that are more granular than the existing four-level government LOAs might help to speed adoption, given that security needs have many different dimensions across the full range of American industry.

A third potential barrier to adoption of authentication technologies is part of a broader cyber security concern: information sharing. Owners and users of information infrastructure may not understand their own vulnerabilities.[29] Without additional information connecting security failures with their ultimate costs, companies are unlikely to invest in better cyber security, and, by extension, better authentication mechanisms.

Finally, even with better information, institutions may not have proper incentives to invest in measures, such as better authentication, that improve cyber security. Some contend that cyber security is a public good and that the private sector may routinely underspend: the costs of security expenditures go directly to the bottom line, but the economic consequences of breaches are diffuse.[30] Under this theory, unless more of the costs of security failures transfer to the institutions that fail to invest in security, adoption of authentication technologies will continue to lag.

Convincing critical infrastructure to adopt appropriate authentication measures is only part of the battle for better authentication. The designers of authentication products also need to focus on making those measures easy to use without reducing their effectiveness. Flaws in protocols and software implementations are sometimes used to foil authentication mechanisms, and authentication manufacturers, like all software manufacturers, need to address those issues as they arise. However, the bigger threat comes from user error. Through the misappropriation of authenticators, malicious actors can gain access to resources they are otherwise unauthorized to use. This information is often exposed by the weakest link in the authentication chain: the individual user.

One way to address this problem might be to increase the interoperability of credentials. When users have a need to access dozens of online retailers and remote servers, each with its own authentication mechanism, the obvious temptation is to create mnemonics: either to duplicate authenticators across providers (e.g., use the same username and password in multiple places) or to store authenticators in an easily accessible location (e.g., put passwords in a text file on a user's desktop).[31] Such mnemonic solutions weaken the strength of authentication measures. If malicious actors can steal lists of authenticators from systems with weak protections or pull a stored list of authenticators off a user machine, they can use the authenticators to compromise a high-security target. It is easier to avoid mnemonics when a user authenticates to a single identity provider, and that provider in turn offers the user's credentials to each relying party. On the other hand, the compromise of an authenticator used across multiple services can have widespread consequences. Too much centralization can be as dangerous as too little. As noted above, the commercial identities most likely to develop toward interoperability are unlikely to be useful in truly sensitive contexts. It is important, therefore, that interoperable systems intended to address these problems are implemented properly: technically secure, privacy-protective, and with appropriate provisions for multiple providers and for anonymous and pseudonymous identification at low LOAs.[32]

The most important ease of use concern, however, may be reducing the possibility of compromise through social engineering and other forms of intelligence collection. Social engineering — the act of manipulating users into turning over confidential information such as authenticators — is a key component of many attacks on authentication mechanisms. By socially engineering users or otherwise collecting information on those users, malicious actors obtain or recreate those users' authenticators without having to crack the authentication system itself. Striking the proper balance between usability and security is a key part of ensuring that authentication measures provide the expected amount of security.[33]

Attribution Concerns.

Even though IP addresses can help to determine physical location in many cases, they often fail to map traffic to a physical identity. Moreover, malicious actors have developed techniques that allow them to obscure their logical identity when sending traffic to a target. Such techniques include identity-stripping, multistage attacks, and multistep attacks.[34] In order to battle these techniques, attributors would need additional information. This information could come from two sources: the collection and sharing of existing information between networks on the larger Internet, and the creation and collection of additional information connecting both logical and physical identities to incoming traffic.

Although IP addresses can be helpful in narrowing down a communicant's location, an Internet-facing IP address does not easily map to a particular user. In various situations, users connect to the Internet through systems using Network Address Translation (NAT). Such systems pool traffic on an internal network and stream it out to the Internet using a single Internet-facing IP address. These systems may or may not retain a history of the devices that used the service. Users can also move from local system to local system while continuing to communicate with a traffic recipient, which provides another way to change their IP addresses. Even when records from the right location at the right time can be found, they are likely to map only to a physical hardware address, not a physical user identity.[35]

Sophisticated malicious actors take steps to make attribution through logical addresses even more difficult. When a given attack does not depend on two-way communication, as when a malicious actor attempts to shut down a system by flooding it with traffic (a distributed denial of service attack [DDoS]), that sender may work to remove IP addresses from incoming packets to stymie efforts at attribution. At that point, attributors must trace step-by-step back through packet logs that may or may not exist, and that are often not on machines controlled by the recipient, in order to find the packets' origin.

Even when an attack does require two-way communication, a sender may disguise his logical identity in other ways. Multistage attacks, for example, route through large numbers of servers and/or through networks of compromised computers (botnets). By issuing commands with several intermediate recipients between source and destination, the controller again requires a prospective attributor to trace control information back through those routes. That path will likely include machines that are not part of the recipient's network and that are beyond the easy reach of investigators in the country where the recipient resides. Many multistage attacks also take place in several temporally distinct steps. In other words, over a long period of time, individual machines may be compromised, and the resident malicious software will lie dormant until activated by a controller. Such multistep attacks can make finding the original sender even more difficult, because information required to trace the traffic back to its origin may not have been retained.

These malicious techniques rely on the proposition that tracing traffic through multiple networks is difficult. One possible policy intervention, then, is to increase the ease with which data are shared between networks and between machine owners. However, the number of entities that potentially hold relevant routing data is very large, consisting of essentially every computer connected to the Internet. Creating a trusted network for information sharing even just among the community of ISPs has not proven feasible yet, especially when service providers are in different countries. "[C]ooperation among institutions that possess this data has been slow to emerge" for a number of reasons. [36]

As with the slow adoption of authentication mechanisms, incentives may be part of the problem.[37] Those who possess relevant data may not suffer enough direct damage to make information sharing a priority. Legal barriers to information sharing between ISPs may also play a role. ISPs may fear that sharing such information will run afoul of federal laws on the privacy of communications data.[38] Cautious legal counsel may advise against testing the boundaries of the law. Finally, there may also be technical barriers. Some routers may not currently possess the capabilities required to store traffic information for a significant length of time, or to perform more advanced monitoring of traffic.

Once domestic barriers are addressed, the more challenging problem of sharing traffic information across international borders remains. Law enforcement agencies such as the Federal Bureau of Investigation (FBI) do work across borders to track cybercriminals, and several Western nations have ratified the Budapest Convention, a framework for sharing information related to online crime.[39] However, attempts to create a legal framework that reaches more countries and covers a wider range of cyber security incidents have not progressed.[40] Cyber attacks cross and re-cross borders before reaching their targets. So long as some nations fall outside the network of cooperation, attribution may not be able to proceed further than determining a country of origin.

Going beyond attempts to increase information exchanges, policies could also attempt to create entirely new information trails. The simplest means of doing so would be to implement some of the authentication-oriented changes discussed in the previous section. Attribution is only possible where there is information to audit; instituting new and stronger authentication and authorization mechanisms with associated auditing capabilities and deploying them to critical systems creates that information. Building attribution capabilities into authentication systems is part of the classic network identity and security paradigm known as authentication, authorization, and accountability (AAA).[41] Computer security experts use authentication mechanisms to establish the acceptability of an identity and authorization mechanisms to associate it with actions. Then, through an accounting and logging system, these mechanisms provide records for investigators to retroactively check that identity's use of the system—in other words, to attribute actions.

More fundamental technological changes might include generating more information about traffic as part of the routing process, linking logical identity more tightly to traffic, and even tying physical identity to logical identity through some sort of registration process. All of these methods would create at least some additional information useful to attributors, but the barriers to uniform global cooperation are very high, and the associated technologies could also be subverted by sophisticated malicious actors. Putting such changes into place, though, would also have moderate-to-severe consequences.

PROPOSED SOLUTIONS TO CYBER SECURITY IDENTITY PROBLEMS: WEIGHING THE OPTIONS

Suggestions for solving cyber security identity problems are numerous. This final section lays out some proposals that have been raised in various legislative, technical, and diplomatic forums: first those aimed at authentication issues and then those aimed at attribution issues. This section briefly discusses some of the strengths and weaknesses of each proposal and also sheds light upon any significant effects that policy interventions may have in areas beyond cyber security. Ultimately, the section concludes that authentication-oriented proposals are more likely to create substantial security benefits and less likely to result in undesirable consequences for other values than attribution-oriented proposals, and that policymakers should strongly consider less coercive means of increasing the uptake of successful authentication technologies before turning to regulatory solutions.[42]

Authentication-Related Policy Proposals.

- **Specify or improve cyber security standards, levels of assurance for private-sector systems, and/or metrics for authorization products.** The creation, improvement, and adoption of security standards and metrics for both systems and products can help prioritize the deployment of strong authentication where it is most needed. Such standards could be developed through various processes, involving more or less governmental involvement, and their adoption could be promoted by a variety of means. The White House has suggested that a federally guided process for developing LOAs and metrics would help fill important gaps.[43]

    Without prioritization, any movement toward greater authentication could be chaotic, so better-defined LOAs and metrics would help focus efforts toward securing critical infrastructure first. Ideally, standards and metrics would be industry-created, given the superior understanding of authentication system design in the private sector. Government-created standards or metrics run a risk of ossifying authentication system design because of their potential inflexibility. Given the information deficit in the private sector regarding the nature of the cyber security threat, however, government collaboration in standards design in some capacity seems appropriate.

- **Mandate authentication mechanisms for critical infrastructure**. It may not be sufficient to wait for owners to comply voluntarily with suggested government levels of assurance.[44] Multiple cyber security bills put forward in in a recent session of Congress considered the imposition of regulatory standards on critical infrastructure systems, authority that could encompass standards for authentication.[45]

  Regulation may be capable of pushing strong authentication standards onto critical infrastructure farther and faster than merely voluntary standards and LOAs, assuming that the designated regulator issues regulations in a timely manner and with sufficient specificity. At the same time, regulation in highly technical areas like information security can slow innovation and hold back the adoption of new and better security mechanisms. Moreover, before critical industries can be regulated, they must be defined; some of the recent bills are vague on what systems should be covered.[46]

  Separately, the mandating of authentication may stifle both innovation and free speech rights unless "critical infrastructure" is carefully delimited. While multifactor authentication may be desirable for some factories and power plants, it is inappropriate for the government to demand that many other networked systems, such as communications networks, authenticate their users. Anonymity is a core free speech value,[47] and maintaining the right to anonymity in online communication is critical to keeping that right vital in the digital age.

- **Increase the costs to various parties of breaches caused by the failure to take sufficient security measures.** Increasing the costs of an avoidable security failure to the responsible ISP, network service provider, security software provider, or system operator would increase those parties' willingness to take steps to improve authentication. Cost increases could come in the form of regulatory fines for breach or in tort damages to affected parties. Legal scholars have suggested various ways to shift cost.[48]

  As a practical matter, such approaches may be difficult to implement because of the complexities of determining causation in cyber security breach cases,[49] as well as the difficulties of defining a standard of care. These uncertainties, compounded by innate difficulties in predicting outcomes in the court system or in regulatory processes, may also cause innovation in security technologies to slow as service providers choose only those technologies that are court- or regulator-approved.

- **Enhance federal compatibility with commercial identity infrastructure.** It has been proposed that security in the consumer and e-government contexts could improve by enhancing the interoperability of identity. This is a major theme of the draft National Strategy for Trusted Identities in Cyberspace (NSTIC).[50]

  While the NSTIC is premised on the principle that the private sector should have the lead in the development of identities for access to online services, the federal government might be able to speed adoption of interoperable credentials by relying on commercially issued identities for authenticated transactions with government agencies. The White House strategy recognizes that over-centralization of identity data poses privacy risks. Among other things, identity providers could have a broad window into online behavior. The White House proposal calls for an identity ecosystem that would allow users to move freely between identity providers.[51]

Attribution-Related Policy Proposals.

• **Improve domestic sharing of cyber attack-related information.** Attack traceback is a critical component of attribution and of information-sharing facilitates that traceback. The sharing of cyber security information between ISPs and other network operators in the United States is thus an important step in malicious code analysis and attack prevention, not least because it pools information about attacks that can lead to attribution. The major service providers and network backbone providers already share some information, but have floated proposals that would allow them to share more.[52]

Improving information sharing may require amendments to existing electronic privacy laws, and creating or expanding cyber security information-sharing exceptions will inevitably pose privacy concerns. Narrowly tailoring any new exception could help to minimize the impact on privacy.

- **Improve international sharing of cyber attack-related information.** Information sharing is especially important when international traffic is involved; sharing across borders is the only reliable way to attribute traffic to foreign end users. The Budapest Convention on Cybercrime recognizes this importance: of the seven articles that contain specific obligations for parties, six require cooperation in data retention and information sharing, and the seventh requires a 24-hour point of contact for data requests.[53] However, implementation to date has been limited; even between signatories, sharing is not swift or guaranteed.[54] Broader ratification of the convention and the adoption of a protocol giving more specificity to information-sharing obligations might help.

  However, international information-sharing frameworks that are not carefully designed or do not include adequate standards risk both inadvertent or unjustified sharing of Americans' private data with overseas entities and the possibility that American companies may need to participate in enforcing foreign laws in contravention of U.S. foreign policy goals. Since a large percentage of the world's Internet traffic passes through the United States, a large share of the burden of improved information sharing might fall on U.S.-based service providers. In a larger national security framework, rules that guaranteed information sharing could undesirably tie American hands, given our reported advantages in cyber offense and cyber exploitation.[55]

- **Institute IP traceback mechanisms on a voluntary or mandatory basis.** Some technological solutions to the attribution information deficit have been discussed. One set of solutions involves the implementation of IP traceback mechanisms, which require routers and/or other intermediaries between the sender and recipient of a stream of traffic to send signals periodically to the recipient. In theory, the recipient will ultimately hear from many points along the path that the traffic has traveled, which will assist in reconstructing the path from source to destination.

   There have been a number of proposals for performing IP traceback without redesigning fundamental network protocols.[56] As of May 2008, a working group at the International Telecommunications Union (ITU) was attempting to create a unified IP traceback standard for telecommunications equipment manufacturers.[57] The intermediary use of ITU-standards-compliant routers is voluntary. A regulatory process for critical infrastructure, as proposed in some cyber security bills, could make it mandatory on a domestic basis but, as with other solutions requiring cross-border implementation, the problems of international adoption remain daunting. Also, IP traceback mechanisms beyond simple logging have seen only limited use in the real world. They may be highly effective or trivially avoidable.

   To the extent that IP traceback is effective, it would provide a powerful tool to attributors. It will also present a barrier to the privacy and anonymity of users vis-à-vis both governments and ISPs. While not as dangerous as full-on authentication for all communications networks, IP traceback still provides intermediaries with enough technical know-how a way to trace "undesirable" speech. This would be a powerful tool for governments interested in tracking and stifling dissenters.

For example, as the recent revolutions in Egypt and Libya demonstrated, the Internet is invaluable for organizing and for circumventing government control of other communications channels.[58] One critical component of dissidents' online activities has been the use of tools designed to circumvent government surveillance, many of which are financed, in part, by the U.S. Government.[59] Traceback mechanisms threaten the use of those tools and the safety of those activists.

- **Readdress the Internet along geographical lines.** As the Internet moves from an older version of the IP (IPv4) to a newer one (IPv6), there may be an opportunity to map logical addresses more closely to physical addresses. The larger address space of IPv6 may make it easier to permanently associate some subset of physical devices with fixed logical addresses. It also provides a rare chance to reconsider the procedures for assigning addresses. At least one ITU proposal has suggested that IPv6 addresses be assigned along geographical lines.[60] Again, achieving consistent international implementation seems unlikely, especially when certain government agencies themselves would likely resist being reliably identified.

Pinning logical addresses to devices and/or assigning them geographically would assist in attribution, although careful safeguards would have to be in place to avoid the falsification of addresses (spoofing). Any strong link between IP and physical devices might assist in the persistent tracking of the user of that device, even over multiple Internet sessions, which raises privacy and free speech concerns similar to those discussed in the previous section.

- **Engineer more identity information into packets.** Some technologists have also proposed redesigning the IP or other base protocols to carry more reliable identity information about the sender within each packet. The simplest proposals in this area merely attempt to alter routing information to make spoofing of logical addresses more difficult.[61] Others add device-identifying signatures directly to each packet.[62] Some policymakers have even implied that each packet should link to identity information about the user rather than that user's device, presumably through some sort of authentication mechanism.[63]

Technologists argue that user-focused proposals, in particular, are only marginally helpful in solving attribution problems.[64] Both user- and device-oriented changes to IPs raise market action, innovation, and civil liberties issues. Only heavy subsidies or heavy regulation will persuade institutions and individuals to give up their existing Internet devices. Any Internet-like network that has identity-storing gatekeepers is also a network with significantly higher barriers to entry for innovators, who may now need permission to operate their online services. Such a network would make anonymous speech much more difficult and sharply reduce online privacy.

After examining all of these proposals in the context of their security effects and their effects in other realms, it is clear that there are two major differences between the class of attribution-oriented proposals and the class of authentication-oriented proposals. First, the civil liberties impacts of many of the attribution-oriented proposals may be heavy — the technical proposals, in particular, impact privacy, free speech, and anonymity both at home and abroad — while the civil liberties impacts of the authentication-oriented proposals, if appropriately restricted to critical infrastructure, are lighter. Second, the attribution-oriented proposals address both the creation and deployment of new and unproven technologies, while the authentication-oriented proposals focus mostly on deployment alone, because existing authentication technologies are largely proven.

This suggests that given limited resources, policymakers should focus heavily on authentication-oriented policies as the more effective option for addressing the cyber security identity information deficit. These policies rely on established successful technologies rather than on unproven changes to the fabric of the network, and they carry fewer ancillary concerns for other national values such as civil liberties and innovation. This is so, in large part, because they can target where needed rather than requiring broad-based deployment across communications networks, and therefore the civil liberties penalties fall largely on the limited subset of users who access critical systems rather than the full spectrum of Internet users. Moreover, authentication improvements can also help address attribution concerns as they relate to critical systems — as part of the AAA model of identity and security, authentication can provide the basis for better auditing, which in turn can drive better attribution. By ensuring the deployment of state-of-the-art authentication technologies to critical systems, policymakers may also be able to eliminate a substantial portion of the attribution problem.

Separately, there is a follow-on question as to the right mix of incentives for deploying authentication technologies. Striking the right balance between financial incentives, regulatory commands, and collaborative government-industry standards-setting and research should be the key concern of policymakers. Given the potential economic consequences of the top-down regulatory approach that can backfire, legislators should promote incentives and collaboration as an alternative to regulation where possible.

CONCLUSION

Addressing the identity problems associated with cyber security requires policymakers to distinguish among the various functions of identity technologies, including authentication and attribution. Many proposed solutions aimed at improving online identity for cyber security purposes would impinge on other values. As a result, any attempt to intervene in online identity technologies will demand a careful balancing of costs and benefits, with serious consideration given to that intervention's impacts upon civil liberties, economic freedom, technological innovation, and global discourse. After considering these issues in this more global context, policymakers will find that deploying better authentication technologies to critical infrastructure is the best first step in cyber security identity policy.

ENDNOTES - CHAPTER 6

1. This is not only a civil libertarian perspective. The need to balance competing values has been recognized in the Defense community as well. See *Report of the Defense Science Board Task Force on Defense Biometrics*, Washington, DC: Office of the Undersecretary of Defense for Acquisitions, Technology, and Logistics, March 2007, pp. 70-72.

2. Stephen T. Kent and Lynette I. Millett, eds., *Who Goes There?: Authentication Through the Lens of Privacy*, Washington, DC: National Academies Press, 2003, p. 19. The White House's *National Strategy for Trusted Identities in Cyberspace* (NSTIC) defines authentication as "verifying the identity of a user, process, or device." *National Strategy for Trusted Identities in Cyberspace*, Washington, DC: White House Office of the Cybersecurity Coordinator, April 2011, available from *www.whitehouse.gov/sites/default/files/rss_viewer/NSTICstrategy_041511.pdf* (hereinafter NSTIC), p. 8. See also Committee on National Security Systems, CNSS Instruction No. 4009, *National Information Assurance (IA) Glossary*, 2010, available from *www.cnss.gov/Assets/pdf/cnssi_4009.pdf*, p. 4 (authentication is "the process of verifying the identity or other attributes claimed by or assumed of an entity [user, process, or device], or to verify the source and integrity of data"). For an excellent introduction to authentication, see generally, *Who Goes There?*

3. "Identity" as used in discussions of digital authentication may be different from what we often assume the word means in an offline context. Online identity need not have any connection with real-world identity. See Posting of Kim Cameron to Kim

Cameron's Identity Weblog, July 18, 2007, available from *www.identityblog.com/?p=838* ("digital identity can often just convey that you are a member of some group, or possess some characteristic [for example, your profession, employer, citizenship, role or age]. Similarly, it can indicate that you are the same person who visited a site previously—without conveying any personally identifying information").

4. *Who Goes There?* p. 36.

5. Insecure practices induced by having an unmanageable multiplicity of identity credentials include reusing identities and passwords for both low-security and high-security functions and storing one's hard-to-remember identity credentials in weakly-protected files. Researchers have "observe[d] numerous ways in which the technical failures of lower-security sites can compromise higher-security sites due to the well-established tendency of users to re-use passwords." Joseph Bonneau and Soren Preibush, "The Password Thicket: Technical and Market Failures in Human Authentication on the Web," paper presented at the Ninth Workshop on the Economics. of Infomation Security (WEIS), Boston, MA, June 7, 2010, p. 1. The recent compromise of multiple systems at one consulting firm that provided computer security services exploited a range of such insecure practices. See Peter Bright, "Anonymous Speaks: The Inside Story of the HBGary Hack," *Ars Technica*, February 15, 2011, *arstechnica.com/tech-policy/news/2011/02/anonymous-speaks-the-inside-story-of-the-hbgary-hack.ars.* However, multiuse identities pose their own privacy and security issues, and, unless carefully implemented, can create more problems than they cure. For more detail, see Center for Democracy & Technology (CDT), *Issues for Responsible User-Centric Identity*, 2009, available from *www.cdt.org/files/pdfs/Issues_for_Responsible_UCI.pdf.* Among other concerns, when an individual uses a single identity for different purposes, the compromise of that identity may have far-reaching consequences. *Ibid.*

6. See, e.g., Baris Coskun and Cormac Herley, "Can 'Something You Know' Be Saved?" ISC'08: Proceedings of the 11th International Conference on Information Security, Heidelberg, Germany: Springer-Verlag Berlin, 2008, p. 421 (describing the divide between the three categories); John Brainard *et al.*, "Fourth Factor Authentication: Somebody You Know," ACM Computer and

Communications Security Conference, New York. ACM, 2006, p. 168 (discussing the use of a nontraditional fourth category).

7. For example, Craig Mundie, Chief Research and Strategy Officer at Microsoft, has suggested requiring users to present "Internet drivers' licenses" when accessing the Internet. Steven Yates, "A 'Driver's License' for Internet Users?" *The New American*, February 15, 2010, available from *www.thenewamerican.com/ index.php/tech-mainmenu-30/computers/2945-af-drivers-license-for- internet-users.*

8. For the earliest description of levels of assurance for government systems, see Office of Management and Budget (OMB), Memorandum M-04-04, E-Authentication Guidance for Federal Agencies, Attachment A, 2003, pp. 3-4. "The OMB/NIST 4-level LoA model has been accepted by e-government, e-commerce and research initiatives in several countries." Ning Zhang, *E-infrastructure Security: Levels of Assurance*, London, UK: Joint Information Systems Committee (JISC), 2007, p. 10.

9. *Electronic Authentication Guide: Recommendations of the National Institute of Standards and Technology*, Gaithersburg, MD: National Institute of Standards and Technology, SP 800-63, 2006.

10. The Liberty Alliance released its Identity Assurance Framework in 2008. Press Release, Liberty Alliance, "Liberty Alliance Releases Identity Assurance Framework," June 23, 2008, available from *www.projectliberty.org/news_events/press_releases/ liberty_alliance_releases_identity_assurance_framework/?f=news_ events/press_releases/liberty_alliance_releases_identity_assurance_ framework.* The Liberty Alliance has been absorbed into the Kantara Initiative, which in April 2010 issued an Identity Assurance Framework (IAF) that defers to and adopts the four levels provided by NIST SP 800-63. Kantara Initiative, "Identity Assurance Framework: Assurance Levels," 2010, available from *kantarainitiative.org/confluence/download/attachments/41649275/Kantara+IAF- 1200-Levels+of+Assurance.pdf.*

11. As this suggests, different commercial entities emphasize different aspects of identity. Practitioners of targeted advertising are interested in attribution, while commercial entities engaging in monetary transactions are most concerned with authentication.

A similar split may be found in the cyber security field. Information security officers spend more time implementing authentication, while law enforcement investigators and intelligence collectors and analysts are focused on attribution.

12. See the Kantara Initiative.

13. See Dave Morin, Facebook Developer Blog, May 9, 2008, available from *developers.facebook.com/blog/post/108*.

14. In one recent case, an online gaming service with 12 million subscribers attempted to make players use real names when posting on message boards, only to back down in the face of overwhelming customer criticism. See M. G. Babbage, The Economist Science and Technology Blog, July 13, 2010, available from *www.economist.com/blogs/babbage/2010/07/online_gaming*.

15. There is a relatively new computer security sub-discipline that explicitly addresses the relationship between usability and security. See National Research Council Steering Committee on the Usability, Security, and Privacy of Computer Systems, *Toward Better Usability, Security, and Privacy of Information Technology: Report of a Workshop*, Washington, DC: National Academies Press, 2010.

16. See Jeffrey Hunker, Bob Hutchinson, and Jonathan Margulies, *Roles and Challenges for Sufficient Cyber-Attack Attribution*, Hanover, NH: Dartmouth College, Institute for Information Infrastructure Protection, 2008, available from *www.thei3p.org/docs/publications/whitepaper-attribution.pdf*.

17. Former Director of National Intelligence Mike McConnell has suggested that "deterrence [is] based on a few key elements," with the first being attribution. Mike McConnell, "Mike McConnell on How to Win the Cyber-war We're Losing," *The Washington Post*, February 28, 2010. See also William J. Lynn III, "Defending a New Domain: The Pentagon's Cyberstrategy," *Foreign Affairs*, Vol. 89, No. 5, September-October 2010, p. 97.

18. McConnell suggests "reengineer[ing] the Internet to make attribution, geolocation, intelligence analysis, and impact assessment . . . more manageable." See McConnell.

19. David D. Clarke and Susan Landau, "Untangling Attribution," *Proceedings of a Workshop on Deterring Cyber Attacks*, Washington, DC: National Academies Press, 2010, pp. 25, 31-32 ("Redesigning the Internet so that all actions can be robustly attributed to a person would not help to deter the sophisticated attacks we are seeing today, such as . . . multi-stage attacks. . . .").

20. The U.S. Government has supported anonymity in the service of various national interests. The U.S. Navy helped originate the Tor anonymous routing system to protect communications by military personnel, and domestic law enforcement agencies use it to shield their investigations. The State Department has supported the development and dissemination of anonymization and confidentiality systems for use by human rights activists.

21. International Telecommunications Union (ITU) Study Group 17 on telecommunications security has a subgroup looking at securing ubiquitous telecommunications services such as the Internet. Documents authored by one Chinese member were leaked from this Q6/17 subgroup in September 2008. They refer to use cases for tracing back traffic that include "political opponent[s] to a government publish[ing] articles putting the government in an unfavorable light." Declan McCullagh, "U.N. Agency Eyes Curbs on Internet Anonymity," CNet News, September 12, 2008, available from *news.cnet.com/8301-13578_3-10040152-38.html*. For further discussion of such traceback proposals, see Section IV.

22. See Federal Trade Commission, *Protecting Consumer Privacy in an Era of Rapid Change*, 2010, pp. 63-69 (recognizing potential value in a "Do Not Track" feature for web browsers and sites that would prevent online tracking).

23. IP addresses are assigned by the Internet Assigned Numbers Authority. They are given in blocks to governments, corporations, and regional Internet registries. Those parties rely on their own rules to assign or lease IP addresses to assorted third parties.

24. As noted in Section II, authenticators can include something you know, something you have, or something you are. See note 6 and accompanying text.

25. There are other authentication paradigms, but all rely on secure connections and the exchange of authenticators. For example, web-of-trust authentication requires a trusted third party to vouch for the user. However, this requires the trusted third party to present a key or token establishing his or her identity, which again requires an exchange of authenticators.

26. In a 2010 McAfee survey of executives in seven "critical infrastructure" sectors worldwide, 57 percent reported requiring only a username and password from users logging onto their systems. Stewart Baker, Shaun Waterman, and George Ivanov, *In the Crossfire: Critical Infrastructure in the Age of Cyber War*, McAfee, Inc.: Santa Clara, CA, 2010, p. 34, available from *www.mcafee.com.*

27. See, e.g., James A. Lewis, *Authentication 2.0 — New Opportunities for Online Identification*, Washington, DC: Center for Strategic and International Studies, 2008, p. 1 (noting that "we have very strong credentials that are not widely trusted and therefore not widely used. The problem — and the solution — to authentication do[es] not lie with technology.").

28. See, e.g., OMB Memorandum 04-04, pp. vi-viii (linking each of the four LOAs to a set of technical characteristics of authentication systems that would satisfy those LOAs).

29. According to one 2006 survey of American business practices by the Air Force Research Laboratory, institutions often take action to improve cyber security only when confronted with a particular breach, or when regulatory compliance requires it, rather than engaging in comprehensive cost-benefit analysis. Research Triangle Institute, Economic Analysis of Cybersecurity, Rome, NY: Air Force Research Laboratory, 2006, pp. 13, 64-73.

30. This contention is much debated. Compare Bruce Kobayashi, "Private versus Social Incentives in Cybersecurity: Law and Economics," *The Law and Economics of Cybersecurity*, New York: Cambridge University Press, 2006, pp. 13-28 (arguing that cyber security underspending should be expected, because cyber

security is a public good and because the substantial social harms caused by cyber security breaches are difficult to quantify) with Benjamin Powell, "Is Cybersecurity a Public Good? Evidence From the Financial Services Industry," *Journal of Law, Economics, and Policy*, Vol. 1, Winter 2005 (arguing that there is little empirical evidence that the financial sector underinvests in cyber security).

31. See Bonneau and Preibush.

32. This is, in many ways, the vision of the National Strategy for Trusted Identities in Cyberspace. See NSTIC. See also CDT report on Responsible User-Centric Identity (discussing proper implementation of multiuse identities).

33. See generally NRC report on Better Usability, Security, and Privacy (discussing usability as a security consideration).

34. Multistep and multistage attacks are discussed in greater detail in Clarke and Landau, "Untangling Attribution." In terms of IP address spoofing, the capability to send packets with spoofed addresses remains widespread years after responses to the problem were promulgated. The MIT Spoofer project collects data on the prevalence and efficacy of current best-practice source address validation techniques. The project found in its most recent report that, of clients able to test their provider's source-address filtering rules, 31 percent were able to successfully spoof an arbitrary, routable source address, while 77 percent of clients otherwise unable to spoof could forge an address within their own /24 subnetwork. Robert Beverly *et al.*, "Understanding the Efficacy of Deployed Internet Source Address Validation Filtering," paper presented at the ACM SIGCOMM/USENIX Internet Measurement Conference, Chicago, IL, November 4-6, 2009, p. 1.

35. This is less true when the endpoint system uses authentication. For this kind of last-mile attribution, authentication and auditing can be very helpful. See the latter proposals in Section IV.B for more detail.

36. Aaron Burstein, "An Uneasy Relationship: Cyber Security Information Sharing, Communications Privacy, and the Boundaries of the Firm," paper presented at the Sixth Workshop on the Economics of Information Security (WEIS), Pittsburgh, PA, June 7-8, 2007, p. 2.

37. See note 30 and accompanying text.

38. The relevant exceptions within the Wiretap Act and the Stored Communications Act allow sharing of information when it is a "necessary incident to the rendition of . . . service" or required for the "protection of the rights or property of the provider of that service." See 18 U.S.C. §§ 2511(2)(a)(i) and 2702. Arguably, this does not allow one service provider to share information with another provider when the sharing, however useful to the recipient, is not necessary to the disclosing entity.

39. Convention on Cybercrime, November 23, 2001, CETS 185 (Council of Europe), available from *conventions.coe.int/Treaty/en/ Treaties/Html/185.htm*. The United States is the only non-European nation to have ratified the treaty; Canada, Japan, and South Africa have signed it without ratification.

40. Proposals from both individual nations and UN workgroups have not gained traction. See John Markoff and Andrew E. Kramer, "U.S. and Russia Differ on a Treaty for Cyberspace," *The New York Times*, June 27, 2009, p. A1; Stein Schjolberg, "A Cyberspace Treaty—A United Nations Convention or Protocol on Cybersecurity and Cybercrime, distributed to the United Nations Office on Drugs and Crime," United Nations paper A/Conf.213/ IE/7, March 23, 2010.

41. See, e.g., Authentication, Authorization and Accounting (AAA), Description of Working Group, available from *datatracker. ietf.org/wg/aaa/charter/*.

42. Note that there are cyber security experts on all sides of this debate—some argue attribution is a more pressing identity concern than authentication, while others have focused on authentication. For others, the most serious problem is neither authentication nor attribution, but vulnerable software. Compare McConnell, above, with CSIS Commission on Cybersecurity for the 44th Presidency, *Securing Cyberspace in the 44th Presidency*, Washington, DC, Center for Strategic and International Studies, 2008, pp. 54-55, 61-67 (emphasizing securely authenticated control systems as a key cyber security priority) and with Steven M. Bellovin, SMBlog, July 11, 2010, available from *www.cs.columbia.*

edu/~smb/blog/2010-07/2010-07-11.html. ("The fundamental premise of [the draft NSTIC] is that our serious Internet security problems are due to lack of sufficient authentication. That is demonstrably false. The biggest problem was and is buggy code. All the authentication in the world won't stop a bad guy who goes around the authentication system. . . .") See also "Planning for the Future of Cyber Attack," Testimony Before the House Committee on Science and Technology, Subcommittee On Technology and Innovation, 111th Cong., 2nd sess., July 15, 2010, statement of Robert K. Knake, International Affairs Fellow in Residence, The Council on Foreign Relations ("the problem of attribution has been over-stated for the high end threats that represent a challenge to our national security").

43. See NSTIC, pp. 24-27 (explaining the policy role of the Identity Ecosystem Framework).

44. See CSIS, *Securing Cyberspace*, pp. 61-67.

45. While no bill specifically mentioned authentication, cyber security regulatory provisions allowing the Department of Homeland Security to promulgate mandatory "security measures" were present in bills in both the Senate and House last year. See Protecting Cyberspace as a National Asset Act, S. 3480, 111th Cong. § 248(b) (2010); Homeland Security Cyber and Physical Infrastructure Protection Act, H.R. 6423, 111th Cong. § 224(c) (2010). The leading Senate bill this year is the Cyber Security and Internet Freedom Act, S. 413, which contains identical language to S. 3480 regarding acceptable security measures. At least one authentication product manufacturer called last year for authentication-related regulation to top the list of mandates. See Philip Lieberman, "Applauding the Lieberman-Collins Cyber Security Bill S. 3480," *Identity Week*, June 30, 2010, available from *www.identityweek.com/applauding-the-lieberman-collins-cybersecurity-bill-s-3480/*.

46. See S. 3480 at § 241(4) (defining covered critical infrastructure to include anything "that is a component of the national information infrastructure").

47. See McIntyre v. Ohio Election Commission, 514 U.S. 334, 357 (1995) (calling anonymous speech part of "an honorable tradition of advocacy and dissent" and "a shield from the tyranny of the majority").

48. Data breach notification laws passed in many states appear to have had a "limited impact . . . in pressuring businesses to make fundamental changes in their information security practices." Jane K. Winn, "Security Breach Notification Six Years Later: Are 'Better' Security Breach Notification Laws Possible?" *Berkeley Technology Law Journal*, Vol. 24, No. 3, 2009, p. 1161. See Sasha Romanosky and Alessandro Acquisti, "Security Breach Notification Six Years Later: Privacy Costs and Personal Data Protection: Economic and Legal Perspectives," *Berkeley Technology Law Journal*, Vol. 24, No. 3, 2009, pp. 1094-95. Meanwhile, tort liability for *vendors* of insecure software has been widely proposed but not implemented. See Michael D. Scott, "Tort Liability for Vendors of Insecure Software: Has the Time Finally Come?" *Maryland Law Review*, Vol. 67, No. 2, 2008, pp. 441-42 (briefly describing the history of proposals for a negligence standard for software vendors). Vendors' liability to third parties for breaches of systems running those vendors' software, however, has not yet been the subject of much academic attention. Id. at n.7.

49. See the sources in the previous note. Attribution difficulties also play a part in making the assignment of responsibility in these cases so complex.

50. See NSTIC.

51. See NSTIC, p. 5. (Suggesting users should be able to "choose to obtain [their] credentials from a range of different identity providers, both private and public").

52. See Comments of AT&T, Inc., "In the Matter of Cybersecurity, Innovation, and the Internet Economy Before the Department of Commerce," NTIA, Docket No. 100721305-0305-01, Sep. 20, 2010, pp. 18-20, available from *www.nist.gov/itl/upload/AT-T_Cybersecurity-NOI-Comments_9-20-10.pdf*.

53. See Convention on Cybercrime, art. 29-35.

54. See Council of Europe Project on Cybercrime, Messages from the Octopus Conference, March 20, 2010, pp. 1-2, available from *www.coe.int/t/dghl/cooperation/economiccrime/cybercrime/cy-activity-Interface-2010/2079_IF10_messages_1p%20key%20*

prov%20_26%20mar%2010.pdf (discussing the consensus of participants at the most recent COE conference on combating cybercrime, including statements that "[e]stablishing the Budapest Convention as the global standard goes hand in hand with strengthening the Cybercrime Convention Committee (T-CY) as a forum for information sharing" and that "[a]dditional international standards on law enforcement access to data stored in the 'clouds' may need to be considered").

55. "[E]xecutives from many nations, including many U.S. allies, rank the United States as the country 'of greatest concern' in the context of foreign cyberattacks, just ahead of China." McAfee, *In the Crossfire*, p. 25. It has been reported that the U.S. Government participated in the development of the Stuxnet worm as an alternative to assisting in a physical attack on Iran's nuclear program. See William J. Broad, John Markoff, and David E. Sanger, "Israeli Test on Worm Called Crucial In Iran Nuclear Delay," *The New York Times*, January 16, 2011, p. A1.

56. Most approaches fall into three categories: out-of-band communication between the router and recipient, logging at the router, or in-band communication between the router and recipient via packet modification. See, respectively, Steve Bellovin *et al.*, *ICMP Traceback Messages*, IETF Internet Draft, February 2003, available from *tools.ietf.org/html/draft-ietf-itrace-04*; Alex Snoeren *et al.*, "Single-Packet IP Traceback," *IEEE/ACM Transactions on Networking*, Vol. 10, 2002, p. 721; Stefan Savage *et al.*, "Practical Network Support for IP Traceback," paper presented at ACM SIG-COMM, Stockholm, Sweden, August 28-September 1, 2000.

57. According to one of the few public ITU memos on the subject, the Q 6/17 group referenced supra, note 21, has made IP traceback a "main study item," and a group of editors has been assigned for the last 2 years to work on traceback proposals as a component of future networking equipment standards. See Memorandum from A. M. Rutkowski, Verisign, May 31, 2008, pp. 1-2, available from *www.itu.int/osg/csd/cybersecurity/WSIS/3rd_meeting_docs/Rutkowski_IPtraceback_callerID_rev0.pdf*.

58. See Anne Alexander, "Internet Role in Egypt's Protests," BBC News, February 9, 2011, available from *www.bbc.co.uk/news/world-middle-east-12400319*.

59. See Nicole Gaouette and Brendan Greeley, "U.S. Funds Help Democracy Activists Evade Internet Crackdowns," *Bloomberg News*, April 20, 2011, available from *preview.bloomberg.com/news/2011-04-20/u-s-funds-help-democracy-activists-evade-internet-crackdowns.html*.

60. The then-director of the Telecommunication Standards Bureau of the ITU proposed in 2004 that some portion of the IPv6 address space be allocated to nations, which would then be able to keep more accurate records of the ownership of IP addresses within their IP address blocks. Memorandum of Houlin Zhao, Director of TSB/ITU, to the ITU Council Working Group on WSIS, November 30, 2004, pp. 8-9, available from *www.itu.int/ITU-T/tsb-director/itut-wsis/files/zhao-netgov02.doc*.

61. See David G. Andersen *et al.*, "Accountable Internet Protocol," paper presented at ACM SIGCOMM 2008, Seattle, WA, August 17-22, 2008; Xin Liu *et al.*, "Efficient and Secure Source Authentication with Packet Passports," paper presented at USENIX Steps to Reducing Unwanted Traffic on the Internet, San Jose, CA, July 7, 2006.

62. See Mikhail Afanasyev *et al.*, "Network Support for Privacy-Preserving Forensic Attribution," Communications of the ACM, draft available from *www.thei3p.org/docs/events/WESIIIdentity.pdf*.

63. See McConnell.

64. They note that attribution of multistage attacks, the most serious challenge investigators face, is only marginally addressed by personal identification. Since multistage attacks make use of intermediaries, little additional information would reach the recipient. See Clarke and Landau, "Untangling Attribution," pp. 39-40. They also note there are technical means of subverting any attribution system for sufficiently motivated malicious actors, and therefore, sophisticated actors will continue to falsify their network identity. See Bruce Schneier, "Schneier-Ranum Face-Off: Should We Ban Anonymity on the Internet?" *Information Security*, February 2010. Finally, because sender identification cannot fully address the indirection or falsification problems, they indicate

that any evidence collected by investigators will never be definitive enough or of high enough forensic quality to serve the purposes that make attribution important: criminal investigation and the allocation of responsibility in international cyber attacks. See David D. Clarke and Susan Landau, "The Problem Isn't Attribution; It's Multi-Stage Attacks," paper presented at the Third International Workshop on Re-architecting the Internet (ReArch 2010), Philadelphia, PA, November 2010, pp. 3-4.

CHAPTER 7

EXPLORING THE UTILITY OF OPEN SOURCE DATA TO PREDICT MALICIOUS SOFTWARE CREATION

George W. Burruss
Thomas J. Holt
Adam M. Bossler

A version of this chapter was presented at the annual meeting of the American Society of Criminology in 2009 in Philadelphia, PA, and at the Department of Defense Cybercrime Conference in 2010 in St. Louis, MO. The authors thank Joseph K. Young of Southern Illinois University, Carbondale, for his helpful suggestions about an earlier draft of this chapter.

INTRODUCTION

The information security community has developed a variety of tools to identify and defend against malicious software, though few in the social sciences have explored the environmental and social factors that may affect the creation and distribution of malware. This is due in part to the dearth of available data on the country of origin of malicious software developers and the volume of tools created by hackers across the world. Open source malware repositories exist in online environments, though it is not clear how valid or reliable this information may be to understand the scope of malware. This chapter explored the value of open reporting for malware creation and distribution, and considered how this information may combine with other measures to explore the country-level economic, technological, and social forces that affect the likelihood of malware creation. The findings will improve our understanding of the value of open source data and the prospective influences of macro-level computer crime and hacking in a global context.

Although studies of cybercrime have grown exponentially over the last 2 decades, there are multiple issues regarding the validity and generalizability of cybercrime data.[1] In general, official data on most forms of cybercrime are non-existent, inadequate, or inaccessible to the public.[2] Though various entities in the private sector collect information on certain cybercrimes, malware trends, and specific attacks, they may be unwilling to share that information with researchers because of proprietary methods or information that may be lost.[3] Therefore, most social science scholars interested in the phenomenon of cybercrime collect primary data, often from college students, to understand the scope and predictors of both participation in cybercrime and experiences with victimization. These studies provide useful information on various forms of cybercrime and cyber deviance, such as digital piracy,[4] online harassment,[5] and minor forms of computer hacking.[6] These populations do not, however, appear to engage in the creation of malicious software or more serious forms of computer hacking, which limits our understanding of these phenomena.[7]

For those interested in studying cybercrime at the macro level, data collection and aggregation challenges are even more complex. Cross-national comparisons of crime have been problematic for the study of traditional crimes, since official crime statistics are not available or reliable for many non-Western nations.[8] In addition, reporting crime to law enforcement agencies is not consistent across the world, creating pockets of underreporting. Finally, behaviors are defined and criminalized differently across countries and regions. For example, N. L. Piquero and A. R. Piquero explain that the East and West view intellectual property differently.[9] Developing nations that have desires for continued economic and technological growth may have no interest in passing and/or enforcing legislation protecting intellectual property, as this would otherwise hinder growth and development. As a consequence, cross-national research often examines more traditional and consistently operationalized offenses such as homicide, using data collected by international nongovernmental agencies.[10]

One way that researchers may move beyond the data aggregation issues affecting cybercrime is through the use of data developed in online environments such as web forums, bulletin board systems, and archival websites.[11] The emergence of the Internet enables significant social interactions between individuals across the globe, whether through real-time communications via email, or instant messaging, or asynchronous methods like blogs and texts.[12] As a consequence, researchers can mine these data sources for information to understand cybercrime better, much the same way as traditional ethnographic research on criminal behavior in the real world.

In particular, there are websites that act as online repositories that maintain information on the discovery and description of malicious software and attacks against various resources.[13] Individuals in the hacker community often discuss the tools and resources they find with others in forums and chat rooms in order to gain social status or respect from their peers.[14] Sharing resources may also help elevate an individual's reputation in the digital underground by demonstrating their skill and ability.[15] Furthermore, the computer security community maintains open source repositories of vulnerabilities and exploits—identified in various outlets—to improve awareness of security trends, thereby increasing overall levels of security.[16]

As a consequence, examining these sites can provide practical secondary data sets for social science researchers to understand the potential distribution of malware creators across the globe, the complexity or functionality of these tools, and the influence of various social factors on cybercrime at the macro-level. Data from these repositories can help fill the void left by the lack of reliable and accessible data by the government and private sectors. In addition, these repositories neither rely on governments to report data nor on individuals within a country to report the offensiveness or victimization that has occurred in that country. Instead, interested parties from other countries who have made discoveries can provide information on that software, alleviating many of the problems described and identified in Piquero and Piquero's study of software piracy, regarding cultural definitions of intellectual property and their willingness to protect it.[17] Given the increasing availability and proliferation of open source repositories for information about cybercrimes and attacks in online environments, this study utilized a sample of data developed from one such repository to examine the macro-level predictors of malicious software creation.

LITERATURE REVIEW

The Problem of Malware.

Malicious software systems, or malware, include computer viruses, worms, and Trojan horse programs that can alter functions within computer programs and files, thus enabling attacks against a massive number of targets. Viruses can conceal their presence on computer systems and networks, and can spread via email attachments, downloadable files, instant messaging, and other methods.[18] Trojan horse programs also often arrive via email as a downloadable file or attachment that people would want to open, such as photos, videos, or documents with misleading titles such as "XXX Porn" or "Receipt of Purchase." When the file is opened, it executes some form of malicious code.[19] In addition, some malware is activated by visiting websites, which exploit flaws in web browsers.[20] Though worms do not involve as much user interaction as other malware because of their ability to use system memory and to self-replicate, humans can facilitate their spread by simply opening emails that have the worm code embedded in the file.[21]

The losses associated with malicious software infections and theft are massive, due in part to the costs to remove these programs from a network, declines in productivity among employees and computer systems, and customer apprehension about compromised web pages or online resources.[22] For example, U.S. companies who participated in a recent Computer Security Institute study reported losing an average of $40,000 per respondent due to viruses and $400,000 due to another form of malware called botnet infection.[23] Furthermore, the risk of malicious software is difficult to mitigate, as almost 25 percent of personal computers around the world use a variety of security solutions that have malware loaded into their memory, compared with 33.28 percent of unprotected systems.[24] Thus, malware infection poses a significant threat to Internet users around the globe.

Despite the significant role and utility of malicious software in cybercrime, there is generally little research examining the creators or developers of malware. Individual-level studies suggest that the creators of malware tend to be lone hackers or individuals working in small groups to produce the tools that can be used for financial theft, fraud, or as an instrument to facilitate greater access to computer systems and networks for subsequent attacks.[25] Explorations of the hacker community indicate that hackers exist within a subculture that values profound and deep connections to technology.[26] This subculture is also a meritocracy where others are judged based on their capacity to utilize computers in unique and innovative ways.[27] Access to computer hardware, software, and Internet connectivity varies by place, though there is evidence to suggest hacker communities are present in areas across the emerging world, including North Korea, Central America, and Northern Africa.[28] Thus, one need simply obtain access to computer technology in order to participate within this community.

Hackers are also driven by a variety of motives, particularly status, ego, cause, entry into social groups, and, most notably, economic gain.[29] Hackers also have shifting ethical beliefs about hacking, which concern the consequences of their actions, as demonstrated by their willingness to share hacking, tools and sensitive or fraudulently obtained information in public outlets online.[30] Thus, developing and releasing a highly functional program like a virus, worm, or Trojan horse is a sensible act for a hacker, because he or she may gain respect and status among others, and capitalize on these programs to generate a profit.

Despite the significant risks of hackers and malware to all individuals connected to the Internet, no agreement has been reached worldwide on the best strategies to curtail these problems. For example, the U.S. Computer Fraud and Abuse Act can be used to prosecute the distribution of malicious software through "any computer connected to the Internet, regardless of whether the computers involved are located in the same state."[31] Similar statutes, or models for statutes, such as the United Kingdom (UK) Computer Misuse Act and the Council of Europe Convention on Cybercrime, are in place in industrialized nations to prosecute malware writers and distributors.[32] Emerging industrial nations, however, are less likely to have developed legal guidelines related to malware and other forms of cybercrime.[33] As a result, there are now legal safe havens where malware writers and hackers can operate with minimal risk of extradition and prosecution.[34] For instance, individuals sell services to host malicious software and pornographic materials in Malaysia and other parts of Southeast Asia, where there are fewer legal risks for the buyers, sellers, and operators.[35]

THEORIZING THE STRUCTURAL CORRELATES OF MALWARE CREATION

Though scholars are starting to learn more about hackers and their subculture, little research exists on the macro-level factors that provide a supportive milieu for individuals to develop malicious software. This is problematic, considering that evidence suggests a great deal of modern malware is created and used by computer hackers in foreign countries, particularly China, Russia, Brazil, and Eastern Europe.[36] Few have considered what technological, economic, or social conditions engender the development of malware in these nations, and little to no research considers what forces constrain malware creation. This is a particularly significant issue, given the changing landscape of technology and the economic and social conditions related to access to the Internet and computer resources. As a consequence, it is unclear what factors encourage or hinder malicious software production.

For example, the gross domestic product (GDP) of a nation may have a significant influence on the level of malware produced by a given nation. Specifically, as the economy of a nation improves, this will increase the proliferation of technological infrastructure and resources, which may increase the capacity for actors to become part of the larger international hacker community. Countries with poor economic conditions in comparison to other countries may have less access to high-speed Internet connectivity and powerful computer technology, diminishing the resources available to hackers.[37] A strong economy may also foster a competitive and stable educational system in which computer skills are taught, thus providing a larger labor force with more advanced skills. As long as there is economic growth and stability, individuals with computer skills and training should have access to legitimate jobs within the information technology service sector where many hackers find legitimate employment. Developing nations appear to have an interest in creating and using malicious software that can be applied in information-warfare campaigns against rival nations.[38] Such attacks can be performed with minimal economic investment and low risk of attribution to the originating nation, thereby increasing their overall efficiency. Thus, it is hypothesized that, as GDPs increase, countries become more suitable environments for hackers and the creation of malicious software.

In addition, the number of Internet hosts available in a nation may play a critical role in enabling hackers to create and distribute malware. The global connectivity afforded by the Internet engenders hackers to identify and use resources created by different entities around the world.[39] At the same time, research has noted that substantial hacker communities in Russia, China, and Turkey often utilize web resources created and hosted within their nations as a means of limiting access to outsiders.[40] Thus, if a nation has a larger number of web-hosting resources available, there may be greater opportunities to develop, promote, and share malware and hacking information to their fellow countrymen. This suggests Internet hosting may have a positive impact on the creation of malware.

A country's political system may also influence the production of malware. In theory, one would speculate that democratic or representative government structures, which provide fewer restrictions on individual behavior, would be more likely to encourage innovation and creative efforts. As a consequence, hackers could work covertly to develop resources with less fear of brutal reprisals from the government.[41] However, democratic countries are generally where intellectual property originates, and thus has some of the most stringently enforced intellectual property laws.[42] In addition, totalitarian regimes have historically allowed hackers to attack victims in other nations and

191

have employed or exploited hackers as a means to attack competing democracies.[43] For example, there are a number of reports indicating that hackers with ties to the Chinese military or government have engaged in attacks against the United States and other nations in order to steal sensitive information.[44] Since the identification of individual hackers is difficult, countries can target their enemies through individual hackers without fear of political reprisal. Thus, it is hypothesized that malware will be more often created and utilized in countries with totalitarian regimes than in democratic nations with more political rights.

The ethnic and religious composition of a nation may also affect what countries are more likely to host the creation of malware, but it might affect it on a case-by-case basis. Specifically, a substantial mix of ethnic groups or religions within a nation may cause civil unrest and lead to attacks against different groups within that nation. A predominant ethnic identity within a nation may lead a minority group to utilize hacks and malware as a force multiplier against the government.[45] This is evident in Sri Lanka, where an offshoot of the group the Tamil Tigers uses hacking techniques as a means of disrupting government operations.[46] However, a homogeneous population might simply aim its attacks outwardly rather than inwardly. For example, Turkish hackers frequently attack targets outside of the borders of their Muslim-majority nation.[47] Thus, it is unclear what effect ethnic and religious compositions may have, if any, on malware production.

THE PRESENT STUDY

Despite the significant problems posed by malware, there is little research examining the economic, technological, and social factors that may affect its creation. In this chapter, we propose that online repositories containing data on malicious software can be valuable to study the macro-level correlates of malware creation. If fruitful, this would provide researchers with an additional avenue to study malware specifically and cybercrime generally. Some prospective hypotheses can derive by considering the extant literature on computer hackers and technology adoption. Specifically, environments will be more suitable for the creation of malicious software as GDP and Internet hosts increase in countries governed by regimes that limit political rights. It is unclear how ethnic and religious composition will relate to malware creation. Adopting a similar strategy used by K. Drakos and A. Gafos in their study of transnational terrorists attacks,[48] this study explored the global variation in the production of malicious software through a zero-inflated negative binomial regression (ZINB). In this way, this chapter contributes to the literature by developing an empirical profile of country-level variables that can predict malicious software production while illustrating the usefulness of open source repositories.

DEPENDENT VARIABLE

The data for the dependent variable used for this study (MALWARE) came from an open source malware repository where individuals could post information obtained on malicious software, either because the individual created a program or identified it in the wild.[49] This open source repository provided self-reported information on malware around the globe. In order to report information to the website, an individual would send an email detailing the tool with as much information as possible to the site's director. This repository has been in existence for some time, as it maintains records on malware going back to 2001. Such information would suggest the repository had some recognition in the computer underground and was reputable. It is, however, apparent that self-reporting may undercount the actual number of malicious software produced and released by the hacker community.

Given the range of years available, the dependent variable for this analysis was the number of reported malicious software programs reported in a country in the years 2006, 2007, and 2008 (see Table 7-1 for descriptive statistics). It was necessary to combine multiple years as the number of countries reporting a positive count was extremely low each year: 18, 24, and 18, respectively. Combining these years, however, increased the number of countries with a positive count to 30. This ensured sufficient power for both processes in the ZINB model. Limiting the years included minimized errors due to lagged effects or changes in the predictor variables for these independent variables from 2008.

Many of the malware reports did not identify a country of origin for these tools (50 percent of all). As a result, a number of cases were excluded from the analysis, which may affect the undercounting of countries in this chapter. There is, however, significant difficulty in properly identifying the point of origin for a piece of malicious software.

Number of reported programs	Countries
0	Afghanistan, Albania, Algeria, Andorra, Angola, Antigua and Barbuda, Armenia, Australia, Austria, Azerbaijan, Bahamas, Bahrain, Bangladesh, Barbados, Belarus, Belize, Bhutan, Bolivia, Botswana, Brunei, Burkina Faso, Burma, Burundi, Cambodia, Cameroon, Canada, Chad, Costa Rica, Cote d'Ivoire, Croatia, Cyprus, Czech Republic, Djibouti, Dominica, Dominican Republic, Ecuador, El Salvador, Estonia, Ethiopia, Fiji, Finland, Gambia, Ghana, Greece, Grenada, Guinea, Guinea-Bissau, Guyana, Haiti, , Hungary, Iceland, Indonesia, Ireland, Israel, Japan, Jordan, Kazakhstan, Kenya, Kiribati, South Korea, Kyrgyzstan, Laos, Latvia, Lesotho, Liberia, Libya, Liechtenstein, Lithuania, Luxembourg, Macedonia, Malaysia, Mali, Marshall Islands, Mauritania, Mauritius, Micronesia, Moldova, Mongolia, Mozambique, Namibia, Nauru, Nepal, New Zealand, Nicaragua, Niger, Norway, Pakistan, Panama, Paraguay, Philippines, Samoa, Senegal, Sierra Leone, Singapore, Slovakia, Slovenia, Solomon Islands, Somalia, South Africa, Sri Lanka, Sudan, Swaziland, Switzerland, Taiwan, Tajikistan, Thailand, Togo, Trinidad and Tobago, Turkmenistan, Tuvalu, Uganda, United Arab Emirates, United States, Uruguay, Uzbekistan, Vanuatu, Vietnam, Zimbabwe
1-10	Bosnia Herzegovina, India, Ukraine, United Kingdom, Venezuela, Saudi Arabia, Italy, Peru, Syria, Bulgaria, Chile, Mexico, Argentina, Colombia, Morocco, Spain, Egypt, Tunisia
11-20	Netherlands, Romania
21-50	Belgium, France, Georgia
51-115	Germany, Brazil, Russia, Turkey, Iran, Poland
116-360	China

Table 7-1. Counts of Malicious Software Programs Across Countries.

Specifically, a malware writer may state where he or she created their tool in the program notes, or post their tool directly into this repository providing the necessary information. Some programs may not contain such information, however, and an individual may ascribe an origin point based on the language character set, such as Cyrillic, Chinese, or Western, used in the user interface of the tool kit. While these conditions may affect the validity of the dependent variable, it is still likely that the attributions are accurate and provide some insights into the location of malware creation.

INDEPENDENT VARIABLES

The data for the independent variables derived from the *CIA World FactBook* and from Freedom House, a nongovernmental agency that collects annual data on political freedom around the globe.[50] In order to model the number of reported malicious software programs, we included several co-variates in both the binary and count models. We examined measures on GDP and technological structure, political rights, and population diversity.

In the count model, the first group included measures of GDP and the number of Internet hosts within the country. We used the log of the GDP per capita (*Log GDP*) and the log of Internet hosts (*Log Hosts*), both from the CIA *World Factbook*.[51] We logged the values for these two variables because both distributions were skewed. We also included other measures of technology infrastructure, including the number of cell phones, radio and television stations. However, because these variables all highly correlated with both Log GDP and Log Hosts, we could not include them in the same model.[52] Furthermore, we attempted to include country population as a control variable, but not surprisingly, it was highly correlated with all the predictor variables and also could not be included in the regression model.

The second variable included in the models was the degree of political rights (*political rights*) as measured by Freedom House.[53] The variable ranged from 1 (the most free) to 7 (the least free). Freedom House's measure of political rights is based on a checklist of 10 political rights questions that fall into four subcategories: electoral process, political pluralism, participation, and functioning government. These scores are then used to create the political right subscale.

For measures of diversity, we included two variables: ethnic heterogeneity (*ethnicity*) and religious heterogeneity (*religion*). Both measures derived from the CIA *World Factbook* data, using P. M. Blau's heterogeneity index, calculated as $1 - Pi^2$, where Pi is the proportion of each religious or ethnic group.[54] The squared proportions are summed and subtracted from 1, which gives an index from 0 (total homogeneity) to 1 (total heterogeneity). A higher Blau's index indicated more heterogeneity in the two measures.

Finally, we included a dummy variable for countries on the Asian continent, such as China and North Korea, as a control variable. This variable included Middle Eastern countries such as Iran and Afghanistan as well. Research indicates that Asian countries appear to be a prominent source of malware and hacker activity.[55] In addition, countries with non-Latin alphabets, like China or Iran, might have been more easily detected and have a higher likelihood of being reported in the malware dataset.

COUNT DATA ISSUES: THE ZERO-INFLATED NEGATIVE BINOMIAL MODEL

Our dependent variable (*MALWARE*) reported the count of malicious software detected within each country. Using an ordinary least squares regression

(OLS) was problematic because *MALWARE* was not normally distributed. It was right-tail skewed, as only a few countries reported hundreds of malicious software programs. The remaining countries reported far less than 100, most reporting 0. Thus, the modal count was 0, which resulted in an abundance of 0s in the variable's distribution. In fact, 80 percent of countries reported no malicious software during the study period. Furthermore, the data were reported counts, omitting some countries that undoubtedly produced malicious software, but were not detected by the reporting program. Because of these issues, using OLS regression was likely to result in biased standard errors and coefficients.

To remedy these problems, several limited dependent variable regression models for count data may be employed, including Poisson, zero-inflated Poisson, negative binomial, and zero-inflated negative binomial. A discourse on the differences among these models is beyond the scope of this chapter.[56] Using STATA 8.0, the calculations employed a zero-inflated negative binomial model for two reasons. First, the variance was greater than the mean, resulting in over-dispersion; thus, a Poisson model that assumes equal dispersion was eliminated. Second, the abundant zeros in the frequency distribution likely came from two different groups: the *Always-Zero group* (a country that never produced malicious software) and the *Not-Always-Zero group* (a country that likely produced malicious software).

For example, consider a country from the dataset likely in the *Not-Always-Zero group*. The United States, a technologically advanced country known to have a historically active hacker population,[57] reported zero malicious programs during the study period. The assumption was that this zero count resulted from the reporting process failing to detect malware from the United States. The United States would therefore likely be in the *Not-Always-Zero group*. Since our data did not indicate which group a country belonged to, other than subjective estimation, membership in either of the two zero groups was therefore latent or unobserved. This last point was an important element in favor of a ZINB model, because Poisson or negative binomial models could inflate the probability of a country producing zero programs. The ZINB model predicted membership in either of the two latent groups.

To do this, the ZINB model included two processes in the estimation of the outcome count variable: a binary model and a count model. The binary (or inflated) model, typically logit, predicted the membership of a case in the *Always-Zero group* versus the *Not-Always-Zero group*. The first process accounted for membership in the two groups, while the second count model then predicted the number of counts among countries in the *Not-Always-Zero* group. Both models are reported in the results of a ZINB regression.

The decision to employ a ZINB should be based on the researchers' substantive understanding of how the data were generated, especially when the counts are subject to reporting bias.[58] However, a researcher should also consider the Vuong test.[59] The Vuong statistic can be used to test whether the ZINB model fits the data better than a negative binomial regression. If the Vuong statistic is significant ($V > 1.96$), a ZINB should be employed instead of a negative binomial regression.[60]

The ZINB model then predicted the count of reported malware programs by country based on GDP, Internet hosts, political rights, ethnic heterogeneity, and religious heterogeneity. For the *Always-Zero* inflation model, the study included two predictors: Internet hosts and political rights. Only 30 countries reported malware. Thus, the study minimized inflation in the model to keep it as parsimonious as possible. Given that authoritarian regimes and countries with more Internet hosts are likely producers of malware, these two predictors should confirm or refute current thinking on cross-national production of malware.

FINDINGS

The available data resulted in 147 countries in the sample, which are reported in Table 7-1. The modal count of reported software was zero. Thirty countries reported producing one or more malicious software programs in the sample years. China reported the highest number of software, 353 counts—which is in keeping with emergent research on Chinese hacker activity.[61] It is important to remember that many of the countries in the zero category were actually producers of malware. Such countries likely produced malware in the sample, but they were not detected and reported to the website. Also, it is likely that these countries may have been reported to the website, but the country of origin was not discernible. The ZINB model attempts to replicate the differences in zero counts (i.e. true zeros [no malware] and non-zeros [failure to detect]).

The descriptive statistics for reports of malicious software and the predictor variables appear in Table 7-2. As mentioned previously, the variance of the dependent variable was greater than the mean ($s^2=1108.291$; $m=6.966$), indicating over-dispersion and ruling out a Poisson model. Because GDP and Hosts were logged, their mean levels are difficult to interpret and not as useful, but the values are reported in Table 7-2. The average level of political rights was 3.262, about the middle of the Freedom House scale. The mean levels of religion and ethnic heterogeneity were 0.398 and 0.363, respectively.

Variable	Mean	s.d.	Min	Max
Malware	6.966	33.291	0.000	353
Log GDP	8.796	1.300	5.298	11.282
Log Hosts	10.095	4.261	0.000	19.571
Rights 3.262	2.185	1.000	7.000	
Religion	0.398	0.245	0.000	0.868
Ethnicity	0.363	0.254	0.000	0.950

Table 7-2. Descriptive Statistics (n=147).

Table 7-3 reports the results for the ZINB model. First, the zero-always inflation model reports the likelihood of a country never having reports of malicious software. The results of the Vuong test indicated that the ZINB model was an improvement over a negative binomial model ($V=2.32$; $p< 0.01$). More Internet hosts reduced the likelihood of being in the *Always-Zero group* (b=-1.507). Thus, more hosts increased the likelihood of being malware producers. Fewer political rights also reduced the likelihood of being in the *Always-Zero group* (b=-2.135), meaning that countries with fewer political rights were more likely to have been creators of malware.

Covariate	b	s.e.
Zero-always Inflation Model (Logit)		
Log Hosts	-1.507*	0.720
Political Rights	-2.135*	1.088
Constant	23.443*	10.943
Zero-inflated Negative Binomial Model		
Log GDP	0.054	0.255
Log Hosts	0.504***	0.500
Political Rights	0.297	0.134
Religion	-5.798**	1.786
Ethnicity	-0.658	1.559
Constant	-4.492	5.460
Log Likelihood	-169.844***	
Vuong test	.32*	
Maximum Likelihood R2	0.314	
Notes: * $p<0.5$ ** $p<.01$ *** $p<.001$		

Table 7-3. Zero-inflated Negative Binomial Regression for Count of Malicious Software(n=147).

Separating the two kinds of zero counts into the *Always-Zero* and *Not-Always-Zero groups* allowed us to consider the zero-inflated negative binomial results as presented in Table 7-3. More Internet hosts (logged) increased the number of reported malware programs (b=0.504). Religious heterogeneity was negative, indicating that a more heterogeneous religious milieu reduced the number of reported malware programs (b= -5.798). Log GDP, political rights, and ethnicity were not significant.[62]

A dummy variable was added to control for Asian countries to partially rule out the possibility that countries with a non-Latin alphabet would be more likely to be recognized and reported. Thus, higher counts for Asian countries might have resulted from ease of detection rather than an increased propensity for malware creation. In addition, it was possible that the associations between Internet hosts, political rights, religious heterogeneity, and malware creation were simply due to several Asian countries being high producers of malware. It was therefore important to examine whether these concepts relate to malware generally or whether they were simply descriptive of many Asian countries that happened to be high producers of malware.

The results of this model are reported in Table 7-4. In the *Always-Zero* inflation model, more Internet hosts and less political rights remained significant, both predicting less likelihood of being in the *Always-Zero* model as in the previous model. The dummy variable for Asia was also significant and positive (b= 2.484), indicating that Asian countries were more likely to be in the *Always-Zero* category than non-Asian countries, meaning that they were more likely to not produce it. The dummy Asian measure did not solely account for the relationship between Internet hosts, political rights, and malware, considering that these two measures remained significant in the model. However, it should also be noted that the coefficients decreased substantively between Tables 7-3 and 7-4. This illustrates that the Asian measure did partially mediate the effect of those two measures on malware creation.

Covariate	b	s.e.
Zero-always Inflation Model (Logit)		
Log Hosts	-0.634**	0.213
Political Rights	-0.861*	0.363
Asia	2.483*	1.001
Constant	10.067**	3.392
Zero-inflated Negative Binomial Model		
Log GDP	0.512	0.483
Log Hosts	0.302*	0.500
Political Rights	0.063	0.271
Religion	-3.818*	1.786
Ethnicity	-0.484	1.244
Asia	1.540	0.862
Constant	-5.591	5.719
Log Likelihood	-168.0059**	
Vuong test	1.93*	
Maximum Likelihood R2		
Notes: * $p<0.5$ ** $p<.01$ ***$p<.001$		

Table 7-4. Zero-inflated Negative Binomial Regression for Count of Malicious Software Controlling for Asian Countries (n=147).

In the zero-inflated negative binomial component of the model, the results were similar to the results shown in Table 7-3. Again, only Internet hosts and religious heterogeneity were significant predictors. Thus, the Asia measure did not account for the prediction in reported malware in the count model, either.

In order to make the results more intuitive, predicted counts were calculated for malicious software and the probabilities for being in the *Always-Zero group* from the first regression model (reported in Table 7-3). The results for six countries are reported in Table 7-5. Afghanistan, the first country, had zero reported malware programs during the study period and zero predicted malware programs. The probability for being in the *Always-Zero group* was 0.999. Thus, Afghanistan was correctly classified based on the available data. Next, the United States and Jordan both had zero reported malware programs. The United States was predicted to have 15 reports of malware, while Jordan had only seven. Both countries had very low probabilities of being in the *Always-Zero group*, 0.000 and 0.096 respectively. Finally, three countries had positive observed reports of malware—Turkey (90), Egypt (10), and China (353). Two of the countries, Turkey and Egypt, had about the same number of reported as predicted counts of malware, 96 and 14, respectively. China, however, had far fewer predicted than expected counts (77 versus 353). All three of these countries had zero probability of being in the *Always-Zero group*, and because they were observed to have counts of malware, they were in the negative binomial part of the distribution. These results show how the ZINB regression attempts to model cases where the reported nature of the data produces inaccurate counts.

The probability of having a zero count is also shown in Figure 7-1. The figure shows the change in probabilities of a country having a zero count for each level of political freedom from the most free (1) to the least free (7). All of the other predictor variables are set to their mean values. When zeros from both

Country	Y Count	Ŷ Count	p zero	Distribution
Afghanistan	0	0	.999	Always zero
United States	0	15	.000	Negative binomial
Jordan	0	7	.096	Negative binomial
Turkey	90	96	.000	Negative binomial
Egypt	10	14	.000	Negative binomial
China	353	77	.000	Negative binomial

Notes: Ŷ is the predicted count based on the negative binomial model. The column for 'p zero' is predicted probability that the country is in the *Always-Zero* distribution.

Table 7-5. Observed and Predicted Values for Counts and Probability of Always-Zero Group From Regression Model.

equations are 1.00, the probability of a zero count is 1.00. As countries become less free, the probability of a zero count drops to 0.600. Also, note that in the binary equation that as the level of political freedom approaches its highest value, the probability of a zero in the model drops to zero.

DISCUSSION AND CONCLUSIONS

The diverse and sophisticated threats posed by hackers and malicious software writers require significant investigation by both the technical and social sciences to understand the various forces that affect participation in these activities. It is, however, challenging to identify reliable data sources to examine trends and correlates of malware and hacking events from governmental sources. As a consequence, social

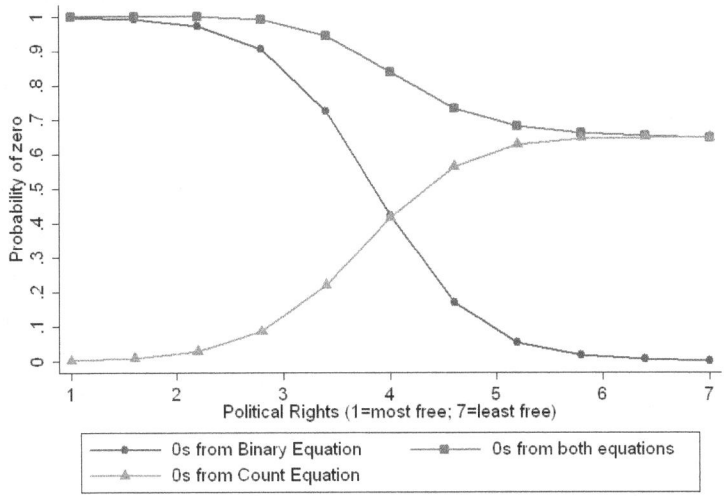

Figure 7-1. Probability of Country Having 0 Reports of Malicious Software by Political Rights.

science research may benefit from data mining online forums and websites to develop data sets.[63] Such efforts may prove beneficial, as online data enable individuals to provide direct information on various forms of cybercrime without stigma or fear that may otherwise result from contacting law enforcement agencies. This study attempted to demonstrate the value of such data through a country-level analysis of the economic, technological, and social forces that affect malware production based on reports to an international online malware repository.

The findings suggest malware production does not depend on a nation's economic conditions unless it affects the development of its technological infrastructure. Those nations with a larger number of Internet hosts were more likely to develop malware resources, because these nations have more opportunities for their citizens to offend. Thus, greater information technology infrastructure may increase the number of people who can go online and increase the development of hacker communities and malware creation.

Considering that GDP did not relate to malware production when controlling for Internet connectivity, this implies that hackers can produce malware with efficiency and can perform this task regardless of legitimate employment opportunities provided by the markets.[64] Additionally, this finding gives some support to the value of malware as a force multiplier in attacks against various targets, as they do not require significant economic investment to be completed. As a result, there may be little policy value to consider how G20 nations are involved in cyber attacks, but rather, to explore the diverse nature of the hacker threat in a global context.[65] For example, understanding the relationships and intersections of hacker communities around the world through online environments may give some insight into the spread of techniques and utilities to develop malware.

This analysis also indicated that more repressive governments created environments in which malware production was more likely. This suggests there is a relationship between political oppression and the development of attack tools. It is unclear, however, if these tools were being created as a means to attack other nations to steal information, engage in espionage, or engage in internal attacks as a means of liberation. The negative effect of religious heterogeneity on malware production, however, suggests that malware was not designed as a means of affecting individuals' religious views within their own country.

The exploratory nature of this chapter provides multiple directions for future research. Specifically, there is a strong need for greater qualitative and quantitative examinations of hacker communities around the world. Research on hacker subcultures in the United States,[66] China,[67] and Russia[68] suggest that there are norms, justifications, and beliefs that drive individual action. Examining the subcultural norms of hacker communities in established and emerging nations in Asia, Northern Africa, and South America can provide insights into the influence of the economic, political, and religious milieu of a nation on hacker activity.

The self-report nature of the data used to develop the dependent variable, malware creation, also suggests a need for further investigation using online data sources on the prevalence and characteristics of malicious software. Many cybercrime scholars have argued for greater official statistics on cybercrime offenses from law enforcement, government agencies, and the private sector.[69] The presence of such published statistics could provide greater insight into the problem of malware, although there is little likelihood that these entities would provide such information to the academic research community. Instead, utilizing data sources such as the information in this analysis provides a necessary and practical alternative to closed sources.

Though there are limitations with the data used in this chapter, as in all self-reporting studies, the work has demonstrated that reporting efforts can be successful in modelling computer crime. The results of this chapter suggest a more concentrated effort by government or academic institutions in collecting self-reported malware production is worth pursuing. Widely publicizing an Internet site where white-hat hackers, Internet security professionals, and laypersons could log detection of malware programs would improve the reliability of the data. Furthermore, such a reporting effort could create a database in which highly visible cyber attacks reported in the media are collected and analyzed, similar to efforts by the University of Maryland's National Consortium for the Study of Terrorism and Responses to Terrorism (START) Center. Given the clandestine nature of hacking, the anonymity of reporters would need to be emphasized and assured to increase participation in reporting. Some kind of verification protocol, such as snippets of code or screenshots of user interface screens, should be implemented to ensure the accuracy of information provided.

Combining this chapter with technical analyses of malware would also allow for some examination of the technical sophistication of the tools created by hackers in each country. Such information could give additional nuance to this study and may demonstrate relationships between the macro-level variables included. For example, if there is a correlation between the production of software designed to steal financial information and the economic or political climate of a nation, this information may help to better understand the drivers for financially motivated cybercrime. Alternatively, examining the programming languages within which these programs are written could be used as a proxy for technical sophistication and skill. If any relationship can be identified between coding languages and technological, economic, or political drivers, such examination may help to better identify the forces that influence malware creation. In turn, this can help to improve understanding of malicious software production at the national level.

ENDNOTES - CHAPTER 7

1. T. J. Holt, "Examining a Transnational Problem: An Analysis of Computer Crime Victimization in Eight Countries from 1999 to 2001," *International Journal of Comparative and Applied Criminal Justice,* Vol. 27, 2003, pp. 199-220; P. N. Grabosky, "Virtual Criminality: Old Wine in New Bottles?" *Social and Legal Studies,* Vol. 10, 2001, pp. 243-249; D. S. Wall, "Catching Cybercriminals: Policing the Internet," *International Review of Law, Computers, & Technology,* Vol. 12, No. 2, 1998, pp. 201-218; H. Stambaugh, D. S. Beaupre, D. J. Icove, R. Baker, W. Cassady, and W. P. Williams, *Electronic Crime Needs Assessment for State and Local Law Enforcement,* Washington, DC, National Institute of Justice.

2. S. W. Brenner, *Cyberthreats: The Emerging Fault Lines of the Nation State,* New York: Oxford University Press, 2008; Holt, "Examining a Transnational Problem"; R. W. Taylor, E. J. Fritsch, J. Liederbach, and T. J. Holt, *Digital Crime and Digital Terrorism,* 2nd Ed., Upper Saddle River, NJ: Pearson Prentice Hall, 2010.

3. *Ibid.*

4. G. E. Higgins, "Can Low Self-Control Help with the Understanding of the Software Piracy Problem?" *Deviant Behavior,* Vol. 26, 2005, pp. 1-24; S. Hinduja, "Trends and Patterns among Online Software Pirates," *Ethics and Information Technology,* Vol. 5, 2003, pp. 49-61; W. F. Skinner and A. M. Fream, "A Social Learning Theory Analysis of Computer Crime Among College Students," *Journal of Research in Crime and Delinquency,* Vol. 34, 1997, pp. 495-518.

5. T. J. Holt and A. M. Bossler, "Examining the Applicability of Lifestyle-Routine Activities Theory for Cybercrime Victimization," *Deviant Behavior,* Vol. 30, 2009, pp. 1-25.

6. A. M. Bossler and G. W. Burruss, "The General Theory of Crime and Computer Hacking: Low Self-Control Hackers?" in T. J. Holt and B. H. Schell, eds., *Corporate Hacking and Technology-Driven Crime: Social Dynamics and Implications,* Hershey, PA: IGI Global, 2011, pp. 38-67; T. J. Holt, G. W. Burruss, and A. M. Bossler, "Social Learning and Cyber Deviance: Examining the Importance of a Full Social Learning Model in the Virtual World," *Journal of Crime and Justice,* Vol. XXXIII, No. 2, 2010, pp. 31-62; M.

Rogers, N. D. Smoak, and J. Liu, "Self-Reported Deviant Computer Behavior: A Big-5, Moral Choice, and Manipulative Exploitive Behavior Analysis," *Deviant Behavior,* Vol. 27, 2006, pp. 245-268; Skinner and Fream, "A Social Learning Theory Analysis of Computer Crime Among College Students."

7. Rogers *et al.*, "Self-Reported Deviant Computer Behavior."

8. G. LaFree, "A Summary and Review of Cross-National Comparative Studies of Homicide," in M. D. Smith and M. A. Zahn, eds., *Homicide: A Sourcebook of Social Research,* Thousand Oaks, CA: Sage Publications, 1999, pp. 125-145; J. L. Neapolitan, *Cross-National Crime: A Research Review and Sourcebook,* Westport, CT: Greenwood Press, 1997.

9. N. L. Piquero and A. R. Piquero, "Democracy and Intellectual Property: Examining Trajectories of Software Piracy," *The Annals of the American Academy of Political and Social Science,* Vol. 605, 2006, pp. 104-127.

10. LaFree, "A Summary and Review of Cross-National Comparative Studies of Homicide;" Neapolitan, *Cross-National Crime.*

11. C. Hine, ed., *Virtual Methods: Issues in Social Research on the Internet,* Oxford, UK: Berg, 2005; T. J. Holt, "Exploring Strategies for Qualitative Criminological and Criminal Justice Inquiry Using On-Line Data," *Journal of Criminal Justice Education,* Vol. 21, 2010, pp. 466-487; G. R. Meyer, *The Social Organization of the Computer Underground,* Unpublished Masters Thesis, 1989, available from *www.csrc.nist.gov/secpubs/hacker.txt.*

12. Hine, *Virtual Methods;* Holt, "Exploring Strategies."

13. T. J. Holt, J. B. Soles, and L. Leslie, "Characterizing Malware Writers and Computer Attackers in Their Own Words," paper presented at the International Conference on Information Warfare and Security, Peter Kiewit Institute, University of Nebraska, Omaha, NE, 2008.

14. The Honeynet Project, *Know Your Enemy: Learning About Security Threats,* Boston, MA: Addison-Wesley, 2001; T. J. Holt, "Subcultural Evolution? Examining the Influences of On- and

Off-Line Experiences on Deviant Subcultures," *Deviant Behavior,* Vol. 28, 2007, pp. 171-198; Meyer, *The Social Organization of the Computer Underground.*

15. *Ibid.*

16. Taylor *et al., Digital Crime and Digital Terrorism.*

17. Piquero and Piquero, "Democracy and Intellectual Property."

18. E. V. Kapersky, *The Classification of Computer Viruses,* Bern, Switzerland: Metropolitan Network BBS Inc., 2003, available from *www.avp.ch/avpve/classes/classes.stm*; P. Szor, *The Art of Computer Virus Research and Defense,* Upper Saddle River, NJ: Addison-Wesley, 2005; Taylor *et al., Digital Crime and Digital Terrorism.*

19. S. Furnell, *Cybercrime: Vandalizing the Information Society,* Boston, MA: Addison-Wesley, 2002; Szor, *The Art of Computer Virus Research and Defense;* Taylor *et al., Digital Crime and Digital Terrorism.*

20. Taylor *et al., Digital Crime and Digital Terrorism.*

21. J. Nazario, *Defense and Detection Strategies Against Internet Worms,* New York: Artech House, 2003.

22. Nazario, *Defense and Detection Strategies Against Internet Worms;* Symantec Corporation, *Symantec Internet Security Report,* 2003, available from *enterprisesecurity.symantec.com/content/knowledgelibrary.cfm?EID=0*; Taylor *et al., Digital Crime and Digital Terrorism.*

23. Computer Security Institute, *Computer Crime and Security Survey,* 2009, available from *www.cybercrime.gov/FBI2009.pdf.*

24. PandaLabs, *Malware Infections in Protected Systems,* 2007, available from *research.pandasecurity.com/blogs/images/wp_bp_malware_infections_in_protected_systems.pdf.*

25. B. Chu, T. J. Holt, and G. J Ahn, *Examining the Creation, Distribution, and Function of Malware On-Line,"* Washington, DC,

National Institute of Justice, 2010, available from *www.ncjrs.gov./ pdffiles1/nij/grants/230112.pdf*; S. Gordon, *Virus and Vulnerability Classification Schemes: Standards and Integration,* Symantec Security Response, 2003, available from *enterprisesecurity.symantec.com/ content/knowledgelibrary.cfm?EID=0*; Holt *et al.,* "Characterizing Malware Writers"; The Honeynet Project, *Know Your Enemy.*

26. Furnell, *Cybercrime*; Holt, "Subcultural Evolution?"; Holt *et al.,* "Characterizing Malware Writers"; T. Jordan and P. A. Taylor, "A Sociology of Hackers," *The Sociological Review,* Vol. 46, 1998, pp. 757-780; P. A. Taylor, *Hackers: Crime in the Digital Sublime,* New York: Routledge, 1999.

27. Holt, "Subcultural Evolution?"; Holt *et al.,* "Characterizing Malware Writers"; The Honeynet Project, *Know Your Enemy*; Jordan and Taylor, "A Sociology of Hackers"; Taylor, *Hackers*; D. Thomas, *Hacker Culture,* Minneapolis, MN: University of Minnesota Press, 2002.

28. C. Brown, *Developing a Reliable Methodology for Assessing the Computer Network Operations Threat of North Korea,* Masters thesis, Monterey, CA: Naval Postgraduate School, 2004; D. E. Denning, "Activism, Hacktivism, and Cyberterrorism: The Internet as a Tool for Influencing Foreign Policy," in J. Arquilla and D. F. Ronfeldt, eds., *Networks and Netwars: The Future of Terror, Crime, and Militancy,* Santa Monica, CA: Rand, 2001.

29. Furnell, *Cybercrime*; Gordon, *Virus and Vulnerability Classification Schemes*; S. Gordon and Q. Ma, *Convergence of Virus Writers and Hackers: Fact or Fantasy?* Cupertine, CA: Symantec, 2003; Holt, "Subcultural Evolution?"; The Honeynet Project, *Know Your Enemy*; L. James, *Phishing Exposed,* Rockland, NJ: Syngress, 2005; Jordan and Taylor, "A Sociology of Hackers"; Taylor, *Hackers*.

30. Furnell, *Cybercrime*; Holt, "Subcultural Evolution?"; T. J. Holt and M. Kilger, "Techcrafters and Makecrafters: A Comparison of Two Population of Hackers," *2008 WOMBAT Workshop on Information Security Threats Data Collection and Sharing,* 2008, pp. 67-78; Holt *et al.,* "Characterizing Malware Writers"; Jordan and Taylor, "A Sociology of Hackers."

31. Brenner, *Cyberthreats*.

32. *Ibid.*; Furnell, *Cybercrime*; Taylor *et al.*, *Digital Crime and Digital Terrorism.*

33. Brenner, *Cyberthreats*; Piquero and Piquero, "Democracy and Intellectual Property"; T. L. Putnam and D. D. Elliott, "International Responses to Cyber Crime," in A. D. Sofaer and S. E. Goodman, eds., *The Transnational Dimension of Cyber Crime and Terrorism,* Stanford, CA: Hoover Institution Press, 2001, pp. 35-68.

34. Brenner, *Cyberthreats*; Putnam and Elliott, "International Responses to Cyber Crime."

35. Chu *et al.*, *Examining the Creation, Distribution, and Function of Malware On-line"*; T. J. Holt and E. Lampke, "Exploring Stolen Data Markets On-Line: Products and Market Forces," *Criminal Justice Studies,* Vol. 23, 2010, pp. 33-50.

36. Chu *et al.*, *Examining the Creation, Distribution, and Function of Malware On-line"*; Denning, "Activism, Hactivism, and Cyberterrorism"; Taylor *et al.*, *Digital Crime and Digital Terrorism;* T. Thomas, "Nation-State Cyber Strategies: Examples from China and Russia," in F. D. Kramer, S. H. Starr, and L. K. Wentz, eds., *Cyberpower and National Security,* Dulles, VA: National Defense University Press, 2009, pp. 465-490; X. Wu, *Chinese Cyber Nationalism: Evolution, Characteristics, and Implications,* Lexington, KY: Lexington Books, 2007.

37. Brown, *Developing a Reliable Methodology for Assessing the Computer Network Operations Threat of North Korea.*

38. Denning, "Activism, Hactivism, and Cyberterrorism"; Taylor *et al.*, *Digital Crime and Digital Terrorism;* Thomas, "Nation-State Cyber Strategies."

39. T. Jordan and P. Taylor, *Hacktivism and Cyberwars: Rebels With a Cause,* New York: Routledge, 2004; Thomas, "Nation-State Cyber Strategies"; D. S. Wall, "Cybercrimes and the Internet," in D. S. Wall, ed., *Crime and the Internet,* New York: Routledge, 2001, pp. 1-17.

40. T. J. Holt, "Chapter 7: The Attack Dynamics of Political and Religiously Motivated Hackers," in T. Saadawi and L. Jordan, eds., *Cyber Infrastructure Protection,* Carlisle, PA: Strategic Studies Institute, U.S. Army War College, 2009, pp. 161-182; Thomas, "Nation-State Cyber Strategies."

41. Jordan and Taylor, "A Sociology of Hackers"; Taylor, *Hackers.*

42. Piquero and Piquero, "Democracy and Intellectual Property."

43. Brenner, *Cyberthreats;* Brown, *Developing a Reliable Methodology;* Thomas, "Nation-State Cyber Strategies."

44. Brenner, *Cyberthreats;* Taylor *et al., Digital Crime and Digital Terrorism;* Thomas, "Nation-State Cyber Strategies."

45. D. T. Kuehl, "From Cyberspace to Cyberpower: Defining the Problem," in F. D. Kramer, S. H. Starr, and L. K. Wentz, eds., *Cyberpower and National Security,* Dulles, VA: National Defense University Press, 2009, pp. 24-43; Taylor *et al., Digital Crime and Digital Terrorism.*

46. Denning, "Activism, Hacktivism, and Cyberterrorism."

47. Holt, "The Attack Dynamics of Political and Religiously Motivated Hackers."

48. K. Drakos and A. Gafos, "In Search of the Average Transnational Terrorist Attack Venue," *Defense and Peace Economics,* Vol. 17, 2006, pp. 73-93.

49. The web address and name of the site are not provided in this analysis in an effort to maintain some confidentiality for the site operator.

50. *The World Factbook 2009;* Washington, DC: Central Intelligence Agency (CIA), 2009, available from *www.cia.gov/library/publications/the-world-factbook/index.html;* Freedom House, *Freedom in the World,* 2008, available from *www.freedomhouse.org.*

51. CIA, *The World Factbook 2009.*

52. While Log Hosts and Log GDP were correlated (r=0.647), the variance inflation factor (VIF) for the regression model indicated no problem with multicollinearity. When the other technology measures were included in the model, multicollinearity would have been an issue.

53. Freedom House, *Freedom in the World*.

54. P. M. Blau, *Inequality and Heterogeneity: A Primitive Theory of Social Structure*, New York: Free Press, 1977.

55. Holt, "The Attack Dynamics of Political and Religiously Motivated Hackers"; Thomas, "Nation-State Cyber Strategies"; Wu, *Chinese Cyber Nationalism*.

56. For a lengthy discussion, see S. Long, *Regression Models for Categorical and Limited Dependent Variables,* Thousand Oaks, CA: Sage Publications, 1997.

57. Holt, "Subcultural Evolution?"; Jordan and Taylor, "A Sociology of Hackers"; Meyer, *The Social Organization of the Computer Underground*.

58. Drakos and Gofas, "In Search of the Average Transnational Terrorist Attack Venue."

59. Long, *Regression Models for Categorical and Limited Dependent Variables*.

60. S. Long and J. Freese, *Regression Models for Categorical and Limited Dependent Variables with Stata,* 2nd Ed., College Station, TX: Stata Press, 2005.

61. Thomas, "Nation-State Cyber Strategies"; Wu, *Chinese Cyber Nationalism*.

62. In a negative binomial model (not shown) that does not include the inflation part of the model, political rights was a significant predictor of reported malware.

63. Holt, "Exploring Strategies for Qualitative Criminological and Criminal Justice Inquiry Using On-line Data."

64. Jordan and Taylor, *Hactivism and Cyberwars;* Taylor, *Hackers.*

65. Holt, "The Attack Dynamics of Political and Religiously Motivated Hackers."

66. Holt, "Subcultural Evolution?"; Meyer, *The Social Organization of the Computer Underground.*

67. Wu, *Chinese Cyber Nationalism.*

68. Chu *et al., Examining the Creation, Distribution, and Function of Malware On-line";* Holt *et al.,* "Characterizing Malware Writers and Computer Attackers in Their Own Words"; A. E. Voiskounsky and O. V. Smyslova, "Flow-based Model of Computer Hackers' Motivation," *CyberPsychology & Behavior,* Vol. 6, 2003, pp. 171-180.

69. Holt, "Examining a Transnational Problem"; Wall, "Catching Cybercriminals"; Grabosky, "Virtual Criminality"; Stambaugh *et al., Electronic Crime Needs Assessment for State and Local Law Enforcement.*

PART III:

CYBER INFRASTRUCTURE

CHAPTER 8

ISP GRADE THREAT MONITORING

Abhrajit Ghosh

INTRODUCTION

Today's Internet Service Provider (ISP) has to deal with various types of threats that impact not only its operations but also those of its customers. These threats manifest in the form of malicious network traffic that may either overload the network infrastructure (e.g., Distributed Denial of Service [DDoS]) or enable the execution of illegal activities (e.g., spam, identity [ID] theft). ISPs can typically provision excess network capacity to deal with volume-based attacks; however, their end customers may not always be able to do so. Consequently, it is very often the ISPs' responsibility to detect and mitigate attacks that target their customers. Originators of malicious activities that are relatively stealthy in nature cannot easily be monitored from their targets, because of the intermittent nature of the activity observed at each individual target. However, an ISP has access to substantially more data on each node within its administrative domain and is in a better position to detect originators of potentially malicious activities, as well as to mitigate the threat posed by them. According to Arbor Networks, the most significant threat faced by IP network operators today is host- or link-level DDoS.[1] A significant portion of DDoS attacks are known to employ IP Spoofing; a technique that allows an attacker to fake source addresses on attack traffic. The use of IP Spoofing makes it more difficult to trace the attack back to its source and delays the start of mitigation. Another significant source of concern is botnet activity. Botnets are networks of (typically) illegitimately controlled computers, spread across the public Internet, under the control of one or more so-called bot-herders. While botnets can be employed for the purpose of originating DDoS attacks, they may also be used to run large spam-delivery operations, which may in turn be used to propagate malicious code onto unsuspecting network users' computers. Botnets can also be used to explore compromised hosts and networks for valuable data to exfiltrate into the hands of an adversary.

Many ISPs operate Security Operation Centers (SOCs), wherein dedicated systems and personnel monitor and analyze data feeds to detect the occurrence of malicious activities. The volume of data available at an ISP's SOC can be challenging for most analysis systems. It is essential that the data collection strategy as well as the analysis algorithms be tuned to such data volumes.

MONITORING FOR THREATS

Several approaches have been proposed in the past for detection of volume-based network attacks. Volume analysis approaches make use of flow record export capabilities at network routers such as sFlow[2] and NetFlow[3] in conjunction with flow-collection software such as nfdump[4] and flow-tools.[5] Analysis algorithms look for evidence of anomalous traffic volumes in the exported flow records. The operation of these components appears in Figure 8-1. Traffic enters a network via one of its edge routers and may traverse one or more core routers before exiting. It is possible to enable flow data export capabilities on either core or edge routers. In many cases, network operators minimize the processing load on routers by mirroring traffic observed at the routers to dedicated flow agents. In the latter case, flow agents act as flow exporters, thus offloading some of the flow data export load from the routers. Exported flow data are directed to one or more flow collectors, which typically save flow information into persistent storage for subsequent analysis. Various flavors of analysis tools are available; for example, nfdump provides tools to compute statistical data on individual flows or on flow aggregates. Tools such as Nfsen provide graphical web-based front ends for flow analysis visualization.[6]

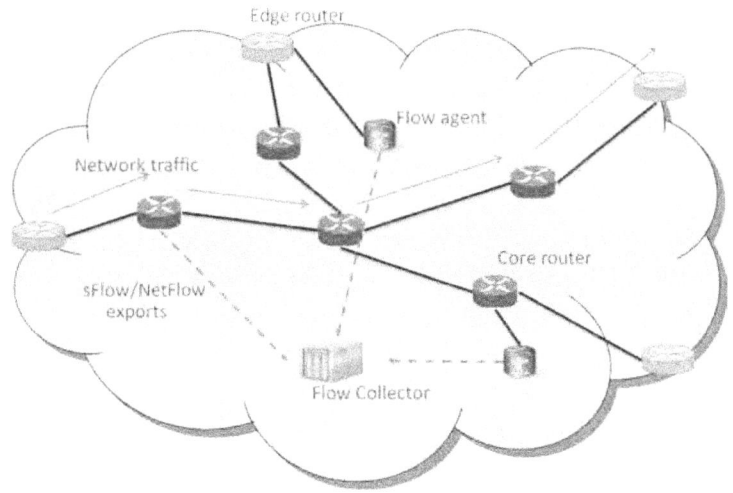

Figure 8-1. Flow Data Collection.

An alternative approach is to use Simple Network Management Protocol (SNMP)-based network monitoring tools to observe standard network monitoring Management Information Bases (MIBs).[7] For example, packets-per-second counters within the

SNMP MIB structure at a router can be used to detect volume anomalies. SNMP-based detection of volume anomalies is inherently coarser grained than the flow analysis-based approaches. On the other hand, SNMP data analysis is a lighter weight process than flow data analysis. Both methods cannot by themselves distinguish between legitimate and illegitimate volume anomalies.

Deep Packet Inspection (DPI)-based approaches provide a means to inspect every byte of every packet passing through the inspection device.[8] This approach allows for the inspection of the application payload the packet carries and can help identify the program or service being used. DPI-based approaches are especially useful for applications that use nonstandard ports such as Skype and other peer-to-peer applications. As such, this is a computationally intensive process, especially at high network data rates, and is typically implemented using custom hardware solutions. The use of custom hardware makes DPI approaches fairly expensive for large-scale deployments. In addition, DPI approaches may not be very useful if the inspected data payloads are encrypted. An approach for using DPI-based solutions is to compare observed application payloads with known attack signatures. However, this requires the maintenance of an attack signature repository and is not very useful when considered in the context of zero-day attacks.

SECURITY MONITORING SYSTEM

Telcordia has spent several years researching various aspects of network security; in particular, the problem of monitoring large-scale networks for malicious activity. The company has developed a system for large-scale security monitoring that examines data exported by flow agents for anomalies. An illustration of a typical deployment appears in Figure 8-2. The system receives NetFlow and sFlow feeds from multiple flow agents located within the monitored network. It also periodically downloads the following types of data from publicly accessible sources:

- BGP (Border Gateway Protocol) routing information from public BGP Routing Information Bases (RIBs).[9]
- BGP Autonomous System (AS) number registration information from Internet Routing Registries (IRRs).[10]
- Blacklisted IP address lists from Domain Name System Blacklists (DNSBLs)[11] and legitimate IP address lists from Domain Name System Whitelists (DNSWLs).[12]

Flow data are analyzed in conjunction with the above types of data sources for anomalies.

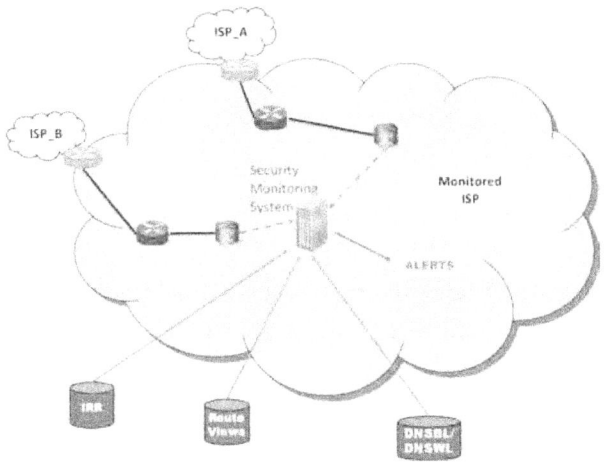

Figure 8-2. Security Monitoring System Deployment.

The goal of the system is to detect various types of network traffic anomalies that could be caused by DDoS, spamming, IP address spoofing, and botnet activities. The system is designed to scale to Tier 1 ISP data rates wherein several gigabytes of flow data could be generated every few minutes.

A high level architecture of the monitoring system appears in Figure 8-3. A set of data collectors acquires flow data from within the monitored network and publicly accessible data from the types of sources listed above that reside outside the monitored network. Collected data are written into persistent storage, which consists of an SQL database and a set of flat files.

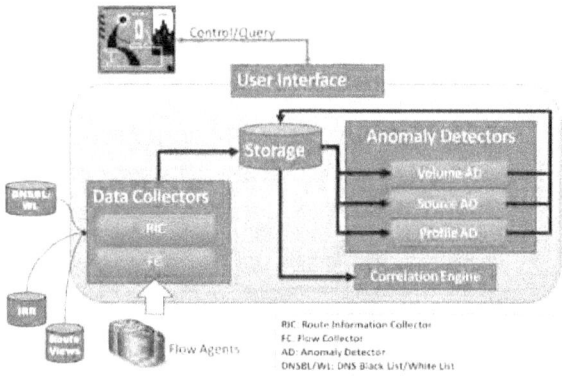

Figure 8-3. Monitoring System Architecture.

A set of anomaly detectors analyzes the collected data and generates alerts when anomalies are detected. Currently three types of anomaly detectors are provided: (a) Volume Anomaly Detectors; (b) Source Anomaly Detectors; and, (c) Profile Anomaly Detectors. The Volume Anomaly Detector analyzes collected data for volume anomalies using a variety of approaches. The Source Anomaly detector incorporates algorithms for spoofed-source IP address detection and makes use of flow data, BGP routing data, and AS number registration data. The Profile Anomaly detector examines the flow-level behavior of individual nodes within the monitored network in conjunction with Blacklist/Whitelist information to identify potentially malicious nodes. Each Anomaly Detector outputs the result of its analysis into a structured query language (SQL) table.

Results of the outputs of various anomaly detectors can be analyzed in conjunction with each other using the Correlation Engine. The Correlation Engine attempts to determine if detected anomalous activities are contemporaneous. It also attempts to identify if an attack source generating one type of attack is also responsible for other types of attacks. As such, the correlation engine provides a means to reduce the overall false-positive rate of the monitoring system.

SECURE ANOMALY DETECTION

The goal of the source anomaly detectors is to identify instances of source IP address spoofing in observed flows. The basic principle of the operation of source anomaly detectors appears in Figure 8-4. Here, data for the monitored ISP are acquired via NetFlow/sFlow data feeds from three flow agents. Source address profiles are generated for each flow agent using training flow data. Alerts are raised when a source IP address that does not match a flow agent's profile is observed at the agent. For example, during training, source IP addresses from ISP_D are expected at flow agent FA2, while source IP addresses from ISP_A are expected at FA1. An alert will occur if flows with source IP addresses from ISP_D are observed at FA1, since this could be evidence of a possible spoofing attack.

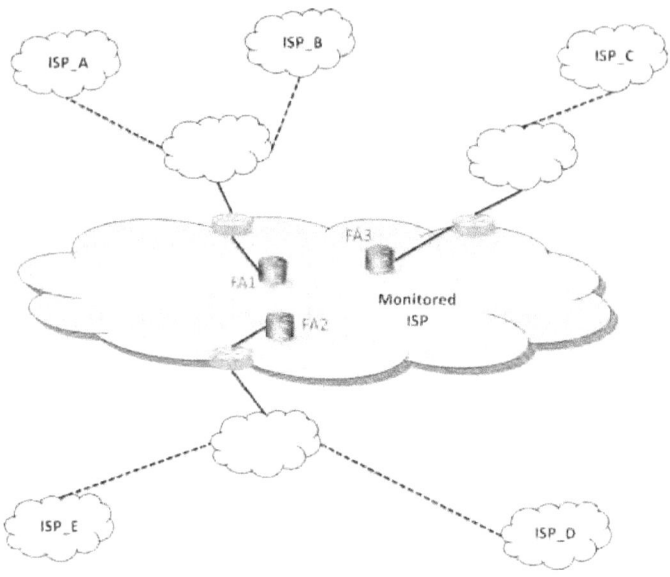

Figure 8-4. Source Anomaly Detection Overview.

While using training data, care must be taken to reduce the possibility of using spoofed traffic to build the source address profiles. While building the profiles, care can be taken by considering only flows for established TCP connections and by ignoring flows to destinations receiving data from bogon sources. It is also possible that training data may not be adequate to cover all potential sources of traffic. One can address this potential issue by considering profiles based on BGP AS numbers, given that a single BGP AS number can map to several IP address prefixes, including those prefixes not observed during training.

PROFILE ANOMALY DETECTION

The profile anomaly detectors detect any behavioral anomalies pertaining to hosts within the monitored network. One profile anomaly detector, that is currently part of the system, identifies potential spammers using flow data and spammer blacklists. Figure 8-5 illustrates the operation of the spammer detector. This detector operates in a two-step process.

1. Training: During this process, training flows build a communication profile for each suspected spammer node. Nodes with similar communication profiles are grouped into clusters. Subsequently, IP address blacklists and whitelists identify clusters that contain known spammers. The existing clusters are then labeled as spammer clusters or as non-spammer clusters.

2. Judgment: As in the training case, observed flows build communication profiles for suspected spammer nodes. The best matching cluster is identified for each communication profile. A node is identified as a spammer if its profile matches a spammer cluster.

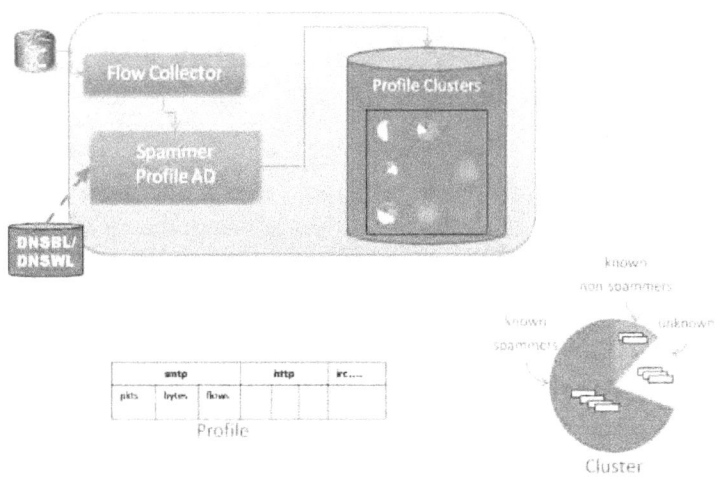

Figure 8-5. Spammer Detection Overview.

VOLUME ANOMALY DETECTION

Our system incorporates an efficient real-time volume anomaly detector that gives early warning of observed volume anomalies. The volume anomaly detector operates by considering a near-term moving window of flow records when computing traffic volumes to a destination address. The operation of the real-time volume anomaly detector appears in Figure 8-6. Flow records from flow agents are stored in memory over a user-defined time window (e.g., 5 minutes). Traffic volumes are computed for destinations observed within a given time window and are compared against operator-specified thresholds to determine the presence of anomalies. This approach eliminates the need to create large archives of flow records for the purpose of volume-based analysis and allows more timely detection of anomalies in the observed data. The approach is also somewhat more accurate than the archive-based approach, since it is not constrained by artificial time boundaries used while archiving files.

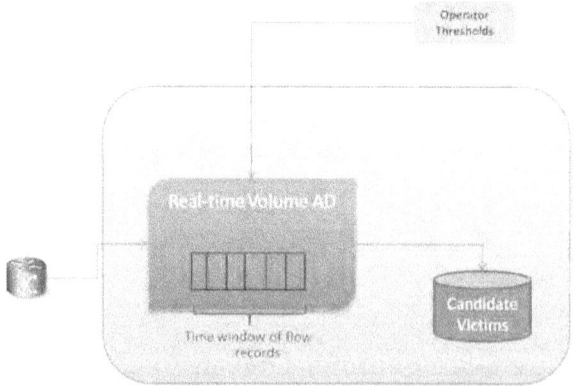

Figure 8-6. Volume Anomaly Detection Overview.

ANOMALY CORRELATION

Our system incorporates a correlation engine that correlates alerts generated by the different types of anomaly detectors. A significant issue with many anomaly detection-based approaches is their potentially high false-positive rate. The correlation engine component reduces the possibility of generating false positives.

Different types of correlations are performed by the system. These may be based on the source IP addresses of observed flows or on their destination IP addresses. For example, source anomaly alerts correlate with volume anomaly alerts to determine whether a volume anomaly targeting a specific destination is happening at the same time as source anomalies are observed. Also, volume anomaly alerts correlate with profile anomaly alerts to determine whether a source of elevated traffic volumes has performed other types of malicious activities such as spamming or participation in a botnet.

CONCLUSION

Our system offers several advantages to an operator who may be interested in monitoring the network for potentially malicious activity. It integrates with standardized data sources, such as NetFlow and sFlow. It has also been evaluated in a Tier 1 ISP environment and has scaled to the high data rates observed therein. There is also no requirement for specialized hardware, as is the case for many current solutions (for example, DPI approaches); the approach is software based and therefore portable.

The use of an alert correlation component is valuable to a network operator who would be very interested in lowering false-positive rates. Given the high data volumes, even a relatively small false-positive rate can lead to a significant number of alerts that may confuse a human operator. This approach uses behavioral anomalies to identify potentially malicious nodes in the target network and is thus in a position to be able to detect zero-day attacks by not depending on the availability of attack signatures. Our system can potentially be used by a network operator to support the delivery of revenue-generating attack detection services to interested customers.

ENDNOTES - CHAPTER 8

1. Arbor Networks, "Worldwide Infrastructure Security Report, Volume V," *www.arbornetworks.com/report*.

2. P. Phaal *et al.*, "InMon Corporation's sFlow: A Method for Monitoring Traffic in Switched and Routed Networks," IETF RFC 3176, September 2001.

3. B. Claise, Ed., "Cisco Systems NetFlow Services Export Version 9," IETF RFC 3954, October 2004.

4. See *nfdump.sourceforge.net/*.

5. See *code.google.com/p/flow-tools/*.

6. See *nfsen.sourceforge.net/*.

7. V. Sekar *et al.*, "LADS: Large-scale Automated DDoS detection System," USENIX Annual Technical Conference, 2006.

8. T. AbuHmed *et al.*, "A Survey on Deep Packet Inspection for Intrusion Detection Systems," *Magazine of Korea Telecommunication Society*, Vol. 24, No. 11, pp. 25-36, November 2007.

9. See *www.routeviews.org/*.

10. See *www.irr.net/*.

11. See *www.uceprotect.net/en/index.php*.

12. See *www.whitelisted.org/*.

CHAPTER 9

THE CHALLEGES ASSOCIATED WITH ASSESSING CYBER ISSUES

Stuart H. Starr

INTRODUCTION

Since the issuance of the 2010 *Quadrennial Defense Review* (QDR), there has been a growing appreciation of the challenges associated with assessing irregular warfare. In particular, there is an understanding that cyber issues are of increased importance in future irregular wars. This manifests in adversary exfiltration of data from sensitive but unclassified databases, cyber attacks on sovereign nations (e.g., Estonia and Georgia), and the fear that critical infrastructures may be the target of a "cyber Pearl Harbor." However, the assessment community is having a difficult time characterizing the current ability to assess cyber issues and prioritizing actions to improve that capability.

The goal of this chapter is to explore the state-of-the-art in the ability to assess cyber issues. To illuminate this problem, the chapter presents a tentative decomposition of the problem into manageable subsets. Using that deconstruction, it identifies candidate cyber policy issues that warrant further analysis and identifies and illustrates candidate Measures of Merit (MoMs). Subsequently, the chapter characterizes some of the more promising existing cyber assessment capabilities that the community is employing, followed by an identification of several cyber assessment capabilities that will be necessary to support future cyber policy assessments. The chapter concludes with a brief identification of high priority cyber assessment efforts to pursue.

DECOMPOSITION OF THE PROBLEM

To structure the problem, the holistic cyber framework is depicted in Figure 9-1. This framework is patterned after the triangular framework that the military operations research community has employed to decompose the dimensions of traditional warfare. In that framework, the base consists of systems models, upon which rests more complex, higher orders of interactions (e.g., engagements, tactical operations, campaigns). Historically, the outputs from the lower levels provide the feedback to the higher levels of the triangle.

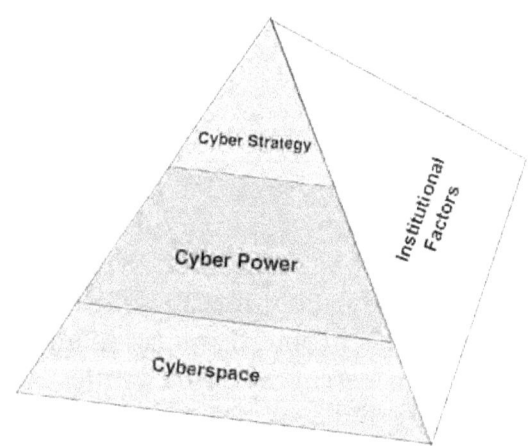

Figure 9-1. Decomposition of the Problem.

By analogy, the bottom of the pyramid consists of "cyberspace," the components, systems, and systems-of-systems that comprise the cyber infrastructure.[1] The output from this cyber infrastructure enhances "cyber power," the traditional instruments of power: political/diplomatic, informational military, and economic (P/DIME).[2] These instruments of power, in turn, provide the basis for "cyber strategy," the empowerment of the entities at the top of the pyramid.[3] These entities include, *inter alia*, individuals, terrorists, transnational criminals, corporations, nation-states, and international organizations. Note that while nation-states have access to all of these instruments of power, the other entities generally have access to only a subset of them. In addition, initiatives, such as deterrence and treaties, may provide the basis for limiting the empowerment of key entities.

The pyramid suggests that each of these levels is affected by institutional factors. These include governance, legal considerations, regulation, critical infrastructure protection, and consideration of civil liberties.

KEY CYBER POLICY ISSUES

Senior decisionmakers have identified several key policy issues that require further attention (see Table 9.1). Note that this list is representative rather than comprehensive. In Table 9.1, these issues have been aggregated into the categories of cyberspace, cyber power, cyber strategy, and institutional factors. Note that most of these issues are extremely broad and contentious. Consequently, new methods, tools, data, and intellectual capital must address them adequately. In particular, there is a need to cast these issues in the proper context so that one can deal with all of the factors of interest.

Category	Key Issues
Cyberspace	What steps should be taken to enhance the **security** of cyberspace?
	What **resources** are needed to make cyberspace resistant to adversary attacks?
Cyber Power	What **risks** does the military face in implementing Net-Centric Operations?
	How **vulnerable** is the network to computer network attack?
	How should Web 2.0 technologies be exploited to enchance **Influence Operations**?
Cyber Strategy	What **norms** should be used among civilized nations?
	What steps should be taken to enhance **cyber deterrence**?
Institutional Factors	When does a cyber attack rise to the level of an **act of war**?
	What **cascading effects** are faced in attacks against critical infrastructures?
	What steps should be **organized** to mitigate cyber risks?

Table 9-1. Selected Cyber Policy Issues.

MEASURES OF MERIT FOR CYBER ISSUES

Table 9-2 suggests a potential decomposition of the MoMs associated with the cyber problem. It identifies four linked sets of measures: Measures of Performance (MoPs), Measures of Functional Performance (MoFPs), Measures of Effectiveness (MoEs), and Measures of Entity Empowerment (MoEEs). Since this field of endeavor is still in its infancy, the material is meant to be illustrative and not exhaustive.

Measures	Representative Measures
Cyber Strategy— Entity Empowerment	• Political reforms (e.g., participation in democratic elections) • Military efforts to enhance security (e.g., reduction in number, severity of insurgent, terrorist attacks) • Economical reforms (e.g., reconstruction projects completed) • Social reforms (e.g., reconciliation of warring parties) • Information (e.g., gaining trust of host nation population) • Infrastructure (e.g., improvement in delivery of electric power, clean water)
Effectiveness (against targeted groups)	• Informational • Media: Number of positive/negative stories published/aired • Clerics: Tone of mosque sermons • Military: Loss Exchange Ratios
Functional Performance	• Informational • Time to create, validate, and disseminate influence messages • Number of meetings held with surrogate groups
Performance	• System performance (e.g., latency, bandwidth, reliability) • Resistance to adversary attack (e.g., ability to withstand a Denial of Service attack)

Table 9-2. Representative Measures of Merit.

MoPs are needed to characterize the key computer science and electrical engineering dimensions of the problem. A key measure is the amount of bandwidth that is available to representative users of cyberspace. As the bandwidth increases to the megahertz/sec range, the user is able to access advanced features such as imagery and video products. A second key measure is connectivity. For circumstances in which the cyber infrastructure is fixed, a useful measure is the percent of people in a country who have access to the Internet. However, in many military operations, the cyber infrastructure and the users are mobile. Under these circumstances, a more useful measure is the performance of Mobile, Ad hoc NETwork (MANET) users (e.g., their ability to stay connected). Third, one can introduce measures of the "noise" that characterizes the cyber infrastructure. For example, the extent to which the quality of the Internet is degraded can be characterized by the unwanted email that it carries ("spam"), which can subsume a substantial subset of the network's capacity. As an example, it has been estimated that in recent months, approximately 90 percent of the traffic on the Internet is spam.[4] In addition, the integrity of the information is further compromised by "phishing" exploits in which criminal elements seek to employ the Internet to perpetrate economic scams. Finally, MoPs can be introduced to characterize resistance to adversary actions, including distributed denial of service (DDoS) attacks, propagation of viruses or worms, and illicitly intruding into a system.

It is useful to introduce MoFPs that characterize how successfully selected entities are able to perform key functions, taking advantage of cyberspace. In the case of the U.S. military, the concept of net-centricity is to employ advances in cyberspace to perform essential functions (e.g., use digital links to disseminate a holistic view of the situation to individual weapon systems). Similarly, a basic tenet of net-centricity is to propagate the commander's intent so that the participants in the operation can synchronize their actions.

MoEs must characterize how effective entities can be in their key missions, taking advantage of cyberspace. In the context of major combat operations, MoEs need to characterize the ability to exploit cyberspace in multiple dimensions. At one extreme, enhancements in cyberspace have the potential to reduce the time to conduct a campaign and the casualties associated with the campaign. At the other extreme, enhancements in cyberspace may substantially enhance blue-loss exchange ratios and the amount of ground gained and controlled.

From the perspective of cyber strategy, there is interest in characterizing the extent to which enhancements in cyberspace can empower key entities. In the case of nation-states, potential MoEEs might include selected political, military, economic, social, informational, and infrastructure (PMESII) variables. As an example, it might address the ability to leverage cyberspace to influence a population (e.g., "win hearts and minds"); shape a nation at strategic crossroads; and deter, persuade, and coerce an adversary.

EXISTING CYBER ASSESSMENT CAPABILITIES

Currently, there are many methods, tools, and data that are being developed to address cyber issues. This section presents a subset of those capabilities in the areas of cyberspace, cyber power, cyber strategy, and institutional factors.

Cyberspace.

In the area of data, we currently have some limited ability to collect real-world cyberspace information. For example, firms such as Gartner, Juniper, Symantec, and IBM extrapolate from samples to estimate the amount of "noise" (e.g., spam) that is infecting the real world. In addition, they provide some limited data characterizing the effectiveness of malware (e.g., DDoS attacks, worms, and viruses).

There are some limited mathematical theories that enable analysts to evaluate the performance of networks. As an illustration, techniques such as percolation theory enable one to evaluate the robustness of a network.[5]

There are also a variety of emerging tools that enable analysts to assess key issues in cyberspace. As a foundation for those tools, operations analysts have historically developed a deep understanding of the nature of the problem by analyzing real operations. In the case of cyber attacks, a representative set of real operations includes the following: Domain Name Server (DNS)-based "pharming attacks" to compromise the DNS server (e.g., redirect the user to a spoofed site or untrusted proxy); email-based "Phishing attacks," in which the phisher might send spam or a targeted email with bait; and deceptive download attacks, in which the adversary piggybacks on other software, posts software on a web site, or corrupts a trusted site.

Similarly, a great deal of useful operational knowledge can derive from key conferences. A representative event is the yearly DEFCON, which bills itself as "the largest underground hacker convention in the world." To suggest its focus, DEFCON has addressed the following issues during 2006 to 2008. In 2006, it focused on "owning" an organization through the BlackBerry and dramatically increasing the "attack surface" through the proliferation of wireless devices (e.g., WiFi) and the transition to IPv6. In 2007, the focus was placed on identity theft. In 2008, the emphasis included exploiting social software, social networks, and hacking opportunities provided by increasing the use of wireless connectivity.[6]

Building on these sources of operational data, there are several modeling and simulation (M&S) tools that the community is employing to address computer science and communications issues. Perhaps the best known simulation is OPNET, which is widely employed to address network architectural issues.[7] However, OPNET and similar tools contain no description of potential vulnerabilities, such as adversary actions, malicious software, or insider threats. A theoretical prediction of the effects of network degradation can be obtained using OPNET (e.g., by the loss of a particular router or host); however, this is not a simulation of an actual threat.

To provide a more controlled environment for analysis, several test beds are emerging. As one example, the iCollege at National Defense University (NDU) has an Information Assurance (IA) Lab. The IA Lab offers detailed opportunities for non-experts to implant malicious code in software applications and operating systems within closed nets using openly available hacking tools.[8] Similarly, the Department of Energy's Pacific Northwest Laboratory is developing a test bed to explore and evaluate alternative cyber-deception strategies.[9] At the other end of the spectrum, the National Research Laboratory (NRL) has developed a Global Information Grid (GIG) Test bed to explore the myriad system-of-systems issues associated with linking new systems and networks.[10]

Cyber Power.

Our primary assessment tools for cyber power deal with the impact of changes in cyberspace on the military and informational levers of national power. In the military domain, interesting tools are emerging in live-virtual-constructive (LVC) simulations. For example, in assessments of air-to-air combat, insights have been derived from the live AIMVAL-

ACEVAL experiments, virtual experiments in the former McDonnell Air Combat Simulator (MACS), and constructive experiments using tools such as TAC BRAWLER and EASDSIM. These studies[11] have enabled researchers to determine that the advantage of a digital link to an airborne interceptor enhances his or her loss-exchange-ratio by approximately 2.5 percent. However, at present, it is not feasible to generate comparable "rules of thumb" for more complex aspects of contemporary warfare (e.g., air-land battle in complex terrain).

More recently, the Information Operations (IO) Joint Munitions Effectiveness Manual (JMEM) is developing frameworks and tools to address the various pillars of IO. These include computer network operations (subsuming Computer Network Attack [CNA], computer network defense, and computer network exploitation), psychological operations (PSYOP), electronic warfare (EW), operations security, and military deception. As an illustration, JMEM is developing a CNA risk-and-effectiveness analyzer (C-REA). This tool uses the effects and response analysis module (ERAM) as its core with interfaces tailored for planners.

In the area of live simulation, the IO range is emerging, with its hub at Cyber Command (CYBER-COM). This links together a variety of existing ranges (e.g., China Lake and Huntsville) to evaluate the use of CNA or EW techniques. Ultimately, the objective is to expand the IO range to evaluate all of the five pillars of IO. However, it is not clear how the existing IO range will evolve to address these other pillars. In addition, DARPA is in the process of developing a national cyber range.

In the informational domain, techniques are emerging to address media effects. One of the major areas of interest for the PSYOP community is to evaluate the effects of media on culture and opinion. To illustrate this interest, there are several tools that have been developed and employed. These include the synthetic environments for analysis and simulation (SEAS), an agent-based model that has been developed by Simulex.[12] JFCOM employed SEAS in Afghanistan to support assessments of the extent to which media broadcasts affected the attitudes of the target population. Similarly, Oak Ridge National Laboratory (ORNL) has developed a tool known as Cultural and Media Influences on Opinion (CAMIO).[13] This tool uses an agent-based approach to assess the opinions of a group and how these opinions can be influenced over time. Representative issues of interest include how small groups of acquaintances form from larger populations and change over time. Furthermore, the IO JMEM has developed effectiveness of psychological influence (EPIC) to support the planning of PSYOP groups in developing and delivering messages.[14] However, in each of these examples, there has not been a rigorous verification and validation (V&V) process.

Looking to the future, there is interest in applying massively multiplayer online games (MMOGs) to informational issues. MMOGs offer a self-organizing environment for strategic communication or social networking that can potentially engage very large populations. A representative MMOG is Second Life. Since it offers the possibility of collecting substantial amounts of socio-behavior data, it has the potential to acquire and analyze tacit knowledge and cultural preferences.

Cyber Strategy.

To support cyber strategy assessments, four key initiatives are being pursued. These include exercises, lessons learned from the real world, new assessment methodologies, and societal models.

Over the last 3 years, the Department of Homeland Security (DHS) has conducted three Cyber Storm national cyber exercises. There is general agreement that these exercises have served to raise awareness of the cyber threat posed to critical infrastructures. However, there is concern that no systematic process exists to transform "lessons recorded" into "lessons learned."

As noted above, operations analysts have been successful when they have effectively derived lessons learned from real-world events. In the area of cyber attack, a substantial amount has been learned from the recent cyber attacks on Estonia and Georgia. In the case of Estonia, an extensive DDoS effectively denied citizens access to key Government sites, financial locations, and the media.[15] In response, Estonia has implemented a NATO Cooperative Cyber Defence Centre of Excellence (CCD COE) to support the planning and response to such attacks. More recently, Russia apparently employed a cyber attack as a precursor to their invasion of Georgia. Although details are sketchy, details are beginning to emerge on the dynamics of that attack.[16]

In response to a recent tasking by STRATCOM, a new methodology and associated tools are emerging to address tailored deterrence issues. The Deterrence Analysis and Planning Support Environment (DAPSE) is a process that is also instantiated in a web application. As part of that process, they have developed a typology (consistent with various social science disciplines) to characterize the information needed for understanding adversaries and other actors of interest. In addition, they have identified a preliminary set of applicable M&S and developed a decision deterrent calculus (DDC) matrix. The DDC matrix identifies perceived feasible/acceptable options by adversaries, potential U.S. options, and the impact of the result on other actors of interest.[17]

Several organizations are in the process of creating and refining societal simulations. As an example, the Systems Architecture Laboratory at GMU has developed a multi-modeling facility. As an element of this tool kit, it uses colored petri nets to create executable models to assess the effect of alternative DIME options on PMESII effects. They attempt to heuristically determine the course of action that maximizes the achievement of desired effects as a function of time.

Furthermore, DARPA's conflict modeling, planning, and outcomes experimentation (COMPOEX) program is developing decision aids to support leaders in designing and conducting future coalition-oriented, multiagency, intervention campaigns employing unified actions, or a whole of government approach to operations.[18] COMPOEX generates a distribution of "plausible outcomes" rather than precise predictions. COMPOEX's components include:

- Conflict Space Tool: This provides leaders and staff with the ability to explore and map sources of instability, relationships, and centers of power to develop their theory of conflict.
- Campaign Planning Tool: A framework to develop, visualize, and manage a comprehensive campaign plan in a complex environment.
- Family of Models: These are instantiated for the current area of responsibility (AoR), based

largely on systems dynamics models.[19] Additional models are being developed to more accurately represent the operational environment for other AoRs.

- Option Exploration Tool: This enables a staff to explore a multiple series of actions in different environments to see the range of possible outcomes in all environments.

However, there are substantial challenges in performing V&V of these tools and transitioning them to operational users.

Institutional Factors.

In the area of institutional factors, primary emphasis has been placed on the development of legal tools and critical infrastructure protection (CIP) tools. In the legal domain, a major challenge is to characterize rapidly whether a cyber attack is an act of war. Michael N. Schmitt of Durham University has developed a framework to address that issue.[20] The framework systematically considers seven factors which are: severity, immediacy, directness, invasiveness, measurability, presumptive legitimacy, and responsibility. Once one has assessed each of those factors, multiattribute utility theory can be employed to weigh each of these factors and come to a determination.

To facilitate legal decisions, a dual-decision tree system has been recommended.[21] The first of these trees is a computer-based tree to assemble key data prior to an actual attack (e.g., primary and secondary levels to characterize international law, constitutional law, executive actions [directives], legislative actions [statutes], or judicial rulings [cases]). This tree is complemented by a human-based tree to support developing a legal brief in near real time, drawing on four levels of abstraction (e.g., citation, precis, excerpt, or full document).[22] Similarly, the system enriches knowledge of legal issues by conducting legal analyses of real-world events (e.g., the NATO CCD COE legal assessment of the Georgian attack).[23]

In the area of CIP, several innovative tools are evolving. The iCollege, NDU, is refining a Supervisory Control and Data Acquisition (SCADA) Laboratory that is designed to explore the vulnerabilities of control systems for electric power generation and other critical infrastructures (e.g., chemical plants or water treatment). Alternatively, under the aegis of DHS, the National Infrastructure Simulation and Analysis Center (NISAC) is developing and applying system dynamics models to assess cascading effects among critical infrastructures. They are taking advantage of the M&S skills resident in Los Alamos National Laboratory and Sandia National Laboratory (LANL/SNL). Furthermore, the U.S. Cyber Consequences Unit (US-CCU) is developing and applying risk assessment tools to critical infrastructure issues. For example, USCCU developed a model of value creation and destruction to evaluate the economic consequences of cyber attacks. In addition, it has published a risk assessment check list for critical infrastructures.[24]

NEEDED CYBER ASSESSMENT CAPABILITIES

This section briefly summarizes some of the major needs for cyber methods, tools, data, and services. In the area of cyberspace, there is a need to institute a more systematic and comprehensive process by which data are collected, organized, and V&V'ed. In addition, there is a need to go beyond OPNET to create a large-scale, high-fidelity model, which can realistically model a set of malicious activities against a real-world network.

In the area of cyber power, there is the need to develop and apply risk assessment tools that enable one to estimate the probability and consequence of a cyber attack. The results can help one prioritize the allocation of resources to support defense of these resources. Second, there is a need to develop additional functional relationships, linking changes in cyberspace to consequences in cyber power. Senior decisionmakers need access to "rules of thumb" that will enable them to assess the impact of changes in cyberspace (e.g., bandwidth, accessibility) to changes in the instruments of power (e.g., the ability to perform diplomatic, informational, military, and economic activities). At this stage, a few limiting cases exist for relatively simple operations (e.g., limited air-to-air combat). A broad set of studies should be performed that are analogous to the activities that were performed (more narrowly) by the Office of Force Transformation.

In the area of cyber strategy, there is the need to extend and apply recently developed methods. In the area of exercises, it is important to go beyond consciousness raising to the development of a process to mitigate identified cyberspace shortfalls. In addition, the method developed by DAPSE may be useful when considering potential options to deter attacks in cyberspace. Furthermore, a great deal of work is required to develop needed cyber strategy tools. First, at the MORS workshop on deterrence,[25] several variants on game theory were identified and discussed to explore contemporary variants on deterrence. It might be useful to develop game-theoretic tools for analyzing potential cyber attacks. Second, most war games lack the fidelity and granularity to explore alternative IO attacks. Activities are underway to identify "best of breed" war games and to identify needed capabilities.[26] Third, there is a need for tools that will support integration across kinetic and nonkinetic attacks. Currently several shortfalls limit the ability to accomplish this objective. For example, in the nonkinetic domain, the IO JMEM activity is developing tools to assess the impact of the individual IO pillars on mission effectiveness. However, there is the need for a capstone tool that will enable tradeoffs across the individual pillars. In addition, there is no tool with adequate scope and granularity to support the formulation and assessment of courses of action that subsume a mix of kinetic and nonkinetic actions.

Fourth, human, social, and cultural behavior (HSCB) will have a major impact on individuals and organizations that are subject to cyber attack. As an example, many of the most successful attacks have cleverly employed social engineering features. Thus, there is a need for a HSCB Modeling Test Bed to evaluate V&V candidate social sciences theories and tools to instantiate those tools. Finally, in the area of societal tools, the system is currently in a very primitive stage. Additional work is required to improve the constituent elements of these tools (e.g., underlying models of economic, political, or social behavior) and their interaction. In particular, there is a need for greater transparency in identifying and tracing cause-and-effect relationships. The HSCB Modeling Test Bed might be a useful mechanism to mature these tools and to perform systematic V&V of them.

Many of the creators of cyber tools lack the knowledge to apply them efficiently and effectively. One of the issues is the large number of variables associated with those tools. To begin to address this issue, two courses of action are necessary. First, flexible, adaptive, and responsive (FAR) exploratory analyses should be performed that develop response surfaces that characterize these tools.[27] Second, innovative experimental designs are required (e.g., exploitation of the insights developed by NPS' SEED Center for Data Farming).[28]

It must be emphasized that virtually none of the tools cited above have undergone rigorous V&V. Even when some of the key V&V tests are performed, they are rarely documented in a clear, transparent fashion that enables senior decisionmakers to make reasoned judgments about the application of these tools to specific issues. The HSCB Modeling Test Bed may prove to be a useful laboratory for conducting these V&V activities.

In the area of institutional factors, there is a need for improved tools to support governance, legal assessments, and CIP issues. Historically, the United States has played a major role in governing cyberspace. However, given the global nature of the Internet, many nations have agitated for a larger role in the governance process. Currently, there is a lack of adequate tools that would enable the formulation and evaluation of key governance issues. As noted above, a proposal has been raised to assemble relevant cyber legal information into dual-decision trees that would enable lawyers to have easy access to key data. An effort is needed to design and instantiate such tools. Finally, as noted above, a number of institutions have been designing and applying a variety of tools to support the assessment of attacks against critical infrastructures (including cascading effects). At this stage, rigorous V&V efforts are required for those tools so that a senior decisionmaker will be able to assign an appropriate level of confidence against those results.

CONCLUSION

This chapter has established a framework for evaluating cyber issues; identified key policy issues that warrant analysis; identified potential MoMs for cyber analysis; characterized the state-of-the-art in performing cyber analyses; and identified key areas that warrant additional attention. As Figure 9-2 suggests, the analysis community's ability to assess cyber issues is uneven. It tends to be strongest in assessing cyberspace issues (in which computer science and electrical engineering issues predominate) and weakest in assessing cyber strategy and institutional factors.

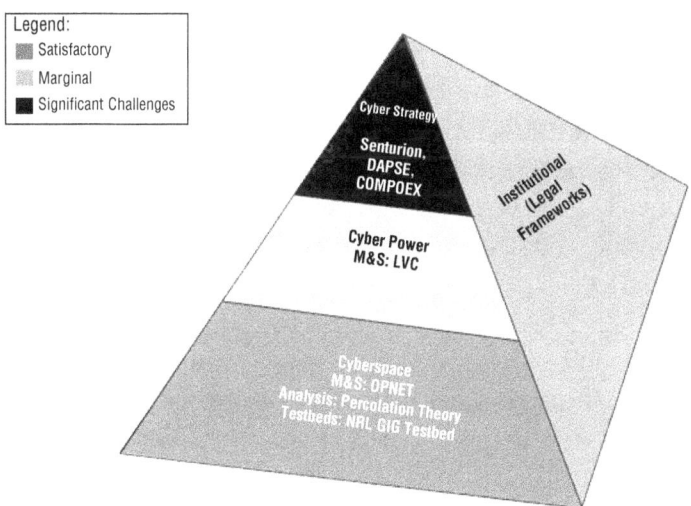

Figure 9-2. Assessment of Existing Cyber Tools.

Overall, there will need to be a substantial infusion of resources to develop the methods, tools, data, and intellectual capital needed to address the concerns of senior decisionmakers. However, given the limited resources that are available, it is suggested that highest priority be given to the following activities. First, although there are interesting individual tools to support the analyses of cyberspace, there is a need for an integrated suite of analysis tools. At the foundation of these tools, actions must be taken to enhance data collection.

Second, the analysis community requires better tools to assess the impact of advances in cyberspace on broader military and informational effectiveness (e.g., land combat in complex terrain). Similarly, tools are necessary to assess the risks that ensue if an adversary is able to compromise net-centric operations. However, there is extensive uncertainty about many of the key parameters that are introduced in the IO JMEMs frameworks (e.g., many of the parameters that characterize the probability of arrival and the probability of damage). This suggests that exploratory analysis techniques be used with these and comparable frameworks, to deal with the massive uncertainty in key parameters. Furthermore, since human responses to cyber actions are of great importance, there is a need for a HSCB Modeling Test Bed to enhance our ability to enhance HSCB modeling.

Third, there is a need to develop tools that explore the impact of alternative mixes of offensive and defensive actions on deterrence strategies. This is extremely important because of recent proposals that have emerged from the White House.[29] Although emerging societal tools are promising, it is vital that they be subject to rigorous validation, verification, and accreditation (VV&A) activities. Finally, there have been a number of studies of cyber attacks against nation-states (e.g., Estonia and Georgia). However, there is a need for a more rigorous assessment to develop and implement lessons learned.

Lastly, several efforts are underway to assess the effectiveness and impact of attacking critical infrastructures. However, if these tools are going to be valuable to senior decisionmakers, it is important that they be subject to rigorous VV&A efforts.

ENDNOTES – CHAPTER 9

1. Cyberspace is defined as: "An operational domain whose distinctive and unique character is framed by the use of electronics and the electromagnetic spectrum to create, store, modify, exchange, and exploit information via interconnected and Internet information systems and their associated infrastructures."

2. Cyber power is defined as "the ability to use cyberspace to create advantages and influence events in the other operational environments and across the instruments of power."

3. Cyber strategy is defined as "the development and employment of capabilities to operate in cyberspace, integrated and coordinated with the other operational domains, to achieve or support the achievement of objectives across the elements of national power."

4. John Soat, "IT Confidential: Is There Anything That Can Be Done About E-mail?" *Information Week*, February 17, 2007.

5. Ira Kohlberg, "Percolation Theory of Coupled Infrastructures," 2007 Homeland Security Symposium, "Cascading Infrastructure Failures: Avoidance and Response," National Academies of Sciences, Washington, DC, May 2007.

6. Linton Wells III, "Understanding Cyber Attacks: Lessons from DEFCON, Georgia and IRMC," CTNSP, NDU, September 22, 2008.

7. Emad Aboelela, "Network Simulation Experiments Manual," Burlington, MA: Morgan Kaufmann, 3rd Ed., June 2003.

8. Wells.

9. "Laboratory for Cyber Deception," Pacific Northwest National Laboratory, Phoenix Challenge 2008, Monterey, CA: Naval Postgraduate School, April 2008, available from *www.pnl.gov/.*

10. Stuart Starr *et al.,* "Concept for an Enterprise Wide, System Engineering Collaborative Engineering Environment," NDIA Systems Engineering Conference, San Diego, CA, October 2006.

11. Daniel Gonzales *et al.,* "Network-Centric Operations Case Study: Air-to-Air Combat With and Without Link 16," Santa Monica, CA: RAND, National Defense Research Institute, 2005.

12. Synthetic Environments for Analysis and Simulation (SEAS), available from *www.simulexinc.com/products/case-studies/.*

13. Cultural and Media Influences on Opinion (CAMIO), available from *www.ioc.ornl.gov/overviews/shtml.*

14. IO Working Group PSYOP Functional Area Working Group, "Where PSYOP JMEM Fits into the PSYOP Planning and Joint Targeting Processes," FA9200-06-C-0024, July 22, 2008.

15. Joshua Davis, "Hackers Take Down the Most Wired Country in Europe," *Wired Magazine,* Issue 15, No. 09, August 21, 2007.

16. The following vignette suggests the ease with which a cyber attack can be launched: Evegny Morozov, founder of the news aggregator Polymeme, categorized his participation in the Georgian cyber attack. "In less than half an hour, drawing on tools available online and a short program he wrote in a Microsoft document, he developed two options to promote DDoS attacks. He then went to a website named 'StopGeorgia,' which claimed to be 'by and for the 'Russian hack underground'." This site provided target lists of websites, with updates as to whether or not they'd already been taken down, and downloadable code to customize attack options that could be launched with a single click on a button labeled "Start Flood." See Wells.

17. Strategic Multi-Layer Analysis Team, Nancy Chesser, ed., "Deterrence in the 21st Century: An Effects-Based Approach in an

Interconnected World, Volume I," sponsored by USSTRATCOM Global Innovation and Strategy Center, October 1, 2007.

18. Ed Waltz, "Situation Analysis and Collaborative Planning for Complex Operations," 13th International Command and Control Research and Technology Symposium (ICCRTS), Bellevue, WA, June 2008.

19. Corey Lofdahl, "Synthesizing Information for Senior Policy Makers Using Simulations," 13th ICCRTS, Bellevue, WA, June 2008.

20. Michael N. Schmitt, "*Bellum Americanum:* The US View of Twenty-first Century War and its Possible Implications for the Law of Armed Conflict," *Michigan Journal of International Law*, Vol. 19, No. 4, 1998, pp. 1051-1090.

21. See Thomas C. Wingfield *et al.*, "Optimizing Lawful Responses to Cyber Intrusions," Paper No. 290, 10th ICCRTS, McLean, VA, June 2005.

22. *Ibid.*

23. Eneken Tikk *et al.*, "Cyber Attacks Against Georgia: Legal Lessons Identified," NATO Cooperative Cyber Defence of Excellence, Tallinn, Estonia, August 2008.

24. John Bumgarner and Scott Borg, "The US-CCU Cyber-Security Check List," Final Version, 2007.

25. "Analytic Tools for Deterrence & Policy Assessment," JHU/APL, Laurel, MD, February 5-7, 2008, MORS, available from *www.mors.org*.

26. Phoenix Challenge Workshop on Information Operations and Wargames, SPAWAR, Charleston, SC, October 28-30, 2008.

27. Thomas L. Allen *et al.*, "Foundation for an Analysis Modeling and Simulation Business Plan," IDA Paper P-4178, December 2007.

28. SEED Center for Data Farming, available from *harvest. nps.edu*.

29. National Security Presidential Directive (NSPD) 54, "On Computer Network Monitoring and Cyber Security," January 8, 2008.

APPENDIX I

ABBREVIATIONS AND ACRONYMS

Abbreviation/ Acronym	Meaning
AoR	Area of Responsibility
CCDCOE	Cooperative Cyber Defense Centre of Excellence
CAMIO	Cultural and Media Influences on Opinion
CIP	Critical Infrastructure Protection
CNA	Computer Network Attack
COMPOEX	Conflict Modeling, Planning & Outcomes Experimentation
C-REA	CNA Risk and Effectiveness Analyzer
DAPSE	Deterrence Analysis and Planning Support Environment
DARPA	Defense Advance Research Project Agency
DDC	Decision Deterrent Calculus
DDoS	Distributed Denial of Service
DHS	Department of Homeland Security
DIME	Diplomatic, Informational, Military, Economic
DNS	Domain Name Server
EADSIM	Extended Air Defense Simulation
EPIC	Effectiveness of Psychological Influence
ERAM	Effects and Response Analysis Module
EW	Electronic Warfare
FAR	Flexible, Adaptable, Robust
GMU	George Mason University
HSCB	Human, Social, Cultural Behavior
IA	Information Assurance
IO	Information Operations
IPv6	Internet Protocol version 6
IRMC	Information Resource Management College
JFCOM	Joint Forces Command

JMEM	Joint Munitions Effectiveness Manual
LANL	Los Alamos National Laboratory
LVC	Live-Virtual-Constructive
M&S	Modeling and Simulation
MACS	McDonnell Air Combat Simulator
MANET	Mobile, Ad hoc, Network
MMOGs	Massively Multiplayer Online Games
MoEs	Measures of Effectiveness
MoEEs	Measures of Entity Empowerment
MoFPs	Measures of Functional Performance
MoMs	Measures of Merit
MoPs	Measures of Performance
MORS	Military Operations Research Society
MTB	Modeling Test Bed
NDU	National Defense University
NISAC	National Infrastructure Simulation and Analysis Center
NPS	Naval Postgraduate School
NRL	Naval Research Laboratory
ORNL	Oak Ridge National Laboratory
PMESII	Political, Military, Economic, Social, Information, and Infrastructure
PSYOP	Psychological Operations
SCADA	Supervisory Control and Data Administration
SEAS	Synthetic Environment for Analysis and Simulation
SEED	Simulation, Experimentation and Efficient Designs
SNL	Sandia National Laboratory
STRATCOM	Strategic Command
US-CCU	U.S. Cyber Consequences Unit
V&V	Verification and Validation
VV&A	Verification, Validation, and Accreditation

ABOUT THE CONTRIBUTORS

ADAM BOSSLER is an assistant professor of justice studies at Georgia Southern University. His research interests include testing criminological theories that have received little empirical testing, such as control balance theory, examining the application of traditional criminological theories to cybercrime for both the offender and the victim, and evaluating policies and programs aimed at reducing youth violence. Dr. Bossler holds a Ph.D. in criminology and criminal justice from the University of Missouri - St. Louis.

VINCENT BOUDREAU is a professor of political science at the City College of New York and at the CUNY Graduate and University Center. He is currently the director of the Colin Powell Center for Leadership and Service at CCNY. Dr. Boudreau is a specialist in the politics of social movements, particularly in Southeast Asia, and his latest book is *Resisting Dictatorship: Repression and Protest in Southeast Asia* (Cambridge University Press). He also conducts research and writes on repression, government transitions to democracy, and collective violence. At CCNY Dr. Boudreau has served as director of the M.A. Program in International Relations, chair of the Department of Political Science, director of the International Studies Program, and deputy dean of the Division of Social Science. In addition to his academic work, he has undertaken projects with ActionAid Asia, Jubilee South Asia, and The Philippine Rural Reconstruction Movement, and has consulted for Oxfam Asia, Action of Economic Reform (Philippines), and Freedom House. Dr. Boudreau holds a Ph.D. from Cornell University.

GEORGE W. BURRUSS is an assistant professor in the Center for the Study of Crime, Delinquency and Corrections, Southern Illinois University, Carbondale. He received his Ph.D. in criminology and criminal justice from the University of Missouri, St. Louis. He does research on criminal justice organizations, including juvenile courts and the police. He has published articles in *Justice Quarterly*, *Policing*, and *Journal of Criminal Justice*.

MELISSA DARK is a professor in computer technology and associate dean in the College of Technology at Purdue. Ms. Dark specializes in educational measurement and evaluation; her measurement and evaluation expertise has been applied to information security for the development of a hacker aptitude test for the Air Force, evaluation models for software security curriculum exercises, and evaluation theory and practice in security education. She has led faculty development projects in technology education and information security education aimed at increasing the knowledge and skills of secondary and post-secondary educators throughout the United States, and has been active in helping define the information assurance discipline. In addition to focusing on educational interventions in information security, Ms. Dark works in information security policy and economics, investigating the impact of both on the socio-technical interface that is at the core of our challenges in information security.

ABHRAJIT GHOSH is a director at Telcordia Technologies. He has extensive research and development experience in the area of cyber security, including network intrusion detection, policy-based network security management, network attack traceback, and secure communication architectures. He is currently leading research activities at Telcordia, addressing ISP level network threat monitoring issues.

JOSHUA GRUENSPECHT is the cyber security fellow at the Center for Democracy and Technology, where he specializes in issues at the intersection of law, privacy norms, and technology. He has also worked on cyber security issues at the Senate Homeland Security Government Affairs Committee, where he was the lead analyst on the Comprehensive National Cyber Security Initiative and drafted legislation to protect the national information infrastructure. Mr. Gruenspecht was also an analyst for computer-related crimes at the Department of Justice. Previously, he was an engineer designing computer network exploitation, network security, and device security solutions, first within the federal government and then with BBN Technologies. Mr. Gruenspecht earned a B.S. in computer science and English at Yale University and a J.D. at Harvard Law School.

THOMAS HOLT is an assistant professor in the School of Criminal Justice at Michigan State University specializing in computer crime, cybercrime, and technology. His research focuses on computer hacking, malware, and the role that technology and the Internet play in facilitating all manner of crime and deviance. Dr. Holt has been published in a variety of academic journals, including *Crime and Delinquency*, *Deviant Behavior,* and the *Journal of Criminal Justice*, and has presented his work at various computer security and criminology conferences. He is the project lead for the Spartan Devils Honeynet Project, which is a joint project of Michigan State University, Arizona State University, and private industry. In addition, he is a member of the editorial board of the International Journal of Cyber Criminology.

LOUIS H. JORDAN, JR., is the Deputy Director of the Strategic Studies Institute, U.S. Army War College, Carlisle Barracks, PA. His assignments include Flight Operations Officer, Company Executive Officer, Asst S3 Air, Asst S3 and Brigade Adjutant in the 42d Infantry (RAINBOW) Division New York Army National Guard. He served as Battalion S3 for 3-140 Aviation (CH-47D), 66th Aviation Brigade, I Corps in Stockton, California. Colonel Jordan has served at the National Guard Bureau as Deputy Division Chief for the Aviation and Safety Division. After serving at the national level, Colonel Jordan commanded the Aviation Support Battalion, Western Army National Guard Aviation Training Site in Marana, Arizona. In 2005, he was selected to be the Brigade Commander for the Western ARNG Aviation Training Site. In 2008, he was selected to command Joint Task Force Raven, the aviation task force for Operation Jump Start along the southwest border in Arizona. Colonel Jordan holds a B.A. in sociology from Fordham University, a master's in strategic studies from the U.S. Army War College, and certification in Strategic Planning from the American Management Association.

DEBORAH WILSON KEELING is currently Chair of the Department of Justice Administration, University of Louisville, KY, and is responsible for academic programs as well as the Southern Police Institute and National Crime Prevention Institute. She has conducted numerous applied research projects for local, state, and federal criminal justice agencies. Dr. Keeling has organized police training programs in the People's Republic of China, Hungary, Romania, and the Republic of Slovakia. She holds a Ph.D. in sociology from Purdue University.

MAX KILGER is a behavioral profiler for the Honeynet Project and contributes additional efforts in the areas of statistical and data analysis. He has written and co-authored research articles and book chapters on the areas of influence in decisionmaking, the interaction of people with technology, the motivations of malicious online actors, and understanding the changing social structure of the computer hacking community. He was the lead author for the Profiling chapter of the Honeynet Project's book, *Know Your Enemy* (2nd Ed.), which serves as a reference guide for information security professionals in government, military, and private sector organizations. Dr. Kilger also co-authored a chapter examining the vulnerabilities and risks of a cyber attack on the U.S. national electrical grid. He recently published a book chapter on social dynamics and the future of technology-driven crime. His most recent publications include two chapters dealing with cyber profiling for Reverse Deception: Organized Cyber Threat Counter-Exploitation (McGraw-Hill). Dr. Kilger was a member of the National Academy of Engineering's Combating Terrorism Committee, which was charged with recommending counterterrorism methodologies to the Congress and relevant federal agencies. He is a frequent national and international speaker to law enforcement, the intelligence community, and military commands, as well as information security forums. Dr. Kilger holds a Ph.D. from Stanford University in social psychology.

MICHAEL LOSAVIO teaches in the Department of Justice Administration and the Department of Computer Engineering and Computer Science at the University of Louisville on issues of law, ethics and society, and information security in the computer engineering and justice administration disciplines. He also works on curriculum development on the use and impact of information and computing systems in a variety of disciplines. Mr. Losavio holds a J.D. in law and a B.S. in mathematics from Louisiana State University.

TAREK SAADAWI is a professor and Director of the Center for Information Networking and Telecommunications (CINT), City College, the City University of New York. His current research interests are telecommunications networks, high-speed networks, multimedia networks, ad hoc mobile wireless networks, and secure communications. He has published extensively in the area of telecommunications and information networks. Dr Saadawi has been on the Consortium Management Committee (CMC) for the Army Research Lab Consortium on Telecommunications (known as Collaborative Technology Alliances on Communications and Networks, CTA-C&N), from 2001 to 2009. Dr. Saadawi is a co-author of the book, *Fundamentals of Telecommunication Networks* (John Wiley & Sons, Inc., 1994), which has been translated into Chinese. He is guest co-editor of the Special Issue on "Mobile Ad-Hoc Wireless Networks," *Journal of Advanced Research*, Vol. 2, Issue 3, July 2011, pp. 195-280. He has been the lead author of the Egypt Telecommunications Infrastructure Master Plan, covering the fiber network, IP/ATM, DSL and the wireless local loop under a project funded by the U.S. Agency for International Development. He has joined the U.S. Department of Commerce delegation to the Government of Algeria addressing rural communications. He is a former Chairman of IEEE Computer Society of New York City (1986-87). Dr. Saawadi holds a B.Sc. and an M.Sc. from Cairo University, Egypt, and a Ph.D. from the University of Maryland, College Park.

J. EAGLE SHUTT is a former prosecutor and public defender and currently is an assistant professor at the Department of Justice Administration, University of Louisville, KY. He also serves as a JAG officer in the South Carolina National Guard. His research interests include biosocial criminology, culture, public policy, and law. Dr. Shutt holds a JD, an MCJ, and a PhD.

STUART STARR is the president of the Barcroft Research Institute (BRI). In that capacity, he consults to government and industry in the areas of command and control assessment, modeling and simulation (M&S), and operations analysis. Prior to founding BRI, he was Director of Plans, MITRE; Assistant Vice President, C2 and Systems Assessment, M/A-COM Government Systems; Director, Long Range Planning and Systems Evaluation, OASD(C3I), OSD, where he was a member of the Senior Executive Service (SES); and Senior Project Leader, Institute for Defense Analyses (IDA). He was a Fellow at MIT's Seminar XXI. Dr. Starr is a Fellow, Military Operations Research Society (MORS); Associate Fellow, AIAA; Member of the Army Science Board; a Senior Research Fellow at the Center for Technology and National Security Policy (CTNSP), National Defense University (NDU); and a frequent participant in Blue Ribbon Panels of NATO, the National Research Council, and the Director, Net Assessment, OSD. Dr. Starr holds a Ph.D. in electrical engineering from the University of Illinois.

www.ingramcontent.com/pod-product-compliance
Lightning Source LLC
Chambersburg PA
CBHW070633290526
45790CB00001B/83